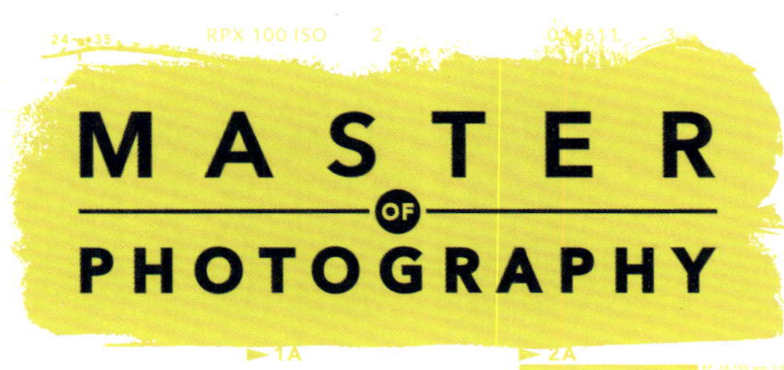

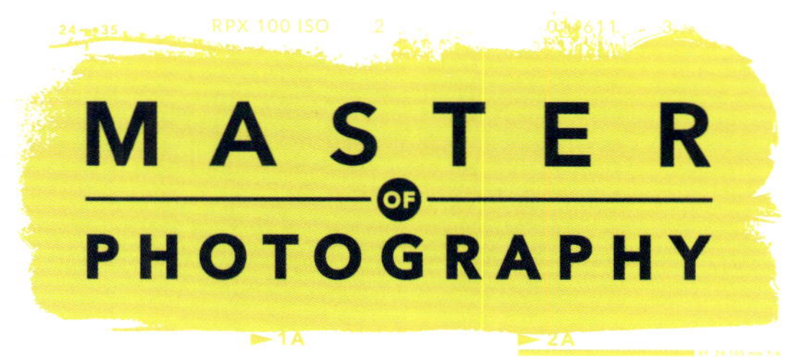

edited by
Filippo Maggia

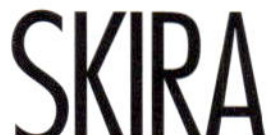

Art Director
Marcello Francone

Design
Luigi Fiore

Editorial coordination
Eva Vanzella

Copy editor
Emanuela Di Lallo

Translation
Lauren Sunstein on behalf
of *Scriptum*, Rome

First published in Italy in 2016 by
Skira editore S.p.A.
Palazzo Casati Stampa
via Torino 61
20123 Milano
Italy
www.skira.net

Printed and bound in Italy.
First edition
ISBN: 978-88-572-3117-4

Distributed in USA, Canada,
Central & South America
by Rizzoli International
Publications, Inc., 300 Park
Avenue South, New York, NY
10010, USA.

Distributed elsewhere in the
world by Thames and Hudson
Ltd., 181A High Holborn,
London WC1V 7QX, United
Kingdom.

Master of Photography

Venice, Fondazione Bevilacqua La Masa
10 September — 9 October 2016

*Exhibition curated
and catalogue edited by*
Filippo Maggia

Texts by
Roberto Pisoni
Filippo Maggia

Graphic direction
Stefano Picarazzi

In collaboration with
Melismelis

We wish to thank
Ballandi Multimedia Srl
Fondazione Bevilacqua La Masa
Comune di Venezia

Exclusive Technical Provider
Leica

A project promoted by

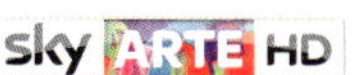
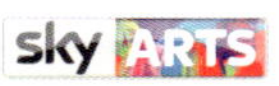
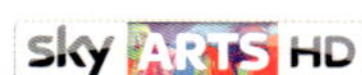

and **Sky Arts Production HUB**

In partnership with

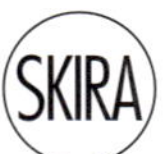

"It is not the person ignorant of writing but the one ignorant of photography who will be the illiterate of the future." So said the great Hungarian painter and photographer László Moholy-Nagy in words later quoted by Walter Benjamin.

Since its launching, Sky Arte channel has always highlighted photography. In fact, this influential means of communication and artistic expression is an enormous reservoir of theories, techniques and stories that deserve to be disseminated, discussed and appreciated in a well-informed way.

For this reason, and in keeping with Sky Arte's lively, contemporary language, we chose to speak of photography through the popular format of the talent show. The result is *Master of Photography*, the first international competition open to photographers from all over Europe in a contest that brings the best of photography and its technical and creative processes directly into homes everywhere.

The project consolidates Sky Arte's wide-ranging collaboration with its European sister channels, creating a competition and a television product that transcends national borders and establishes itself as a model of innovative production and narration for the entire continent.

In an effort to give a unique slant to this talent show, we chose three outstanding judges and an equally exceptional host. Rut Blees Luxemburg, Simon Frederick and Oliviero Toscani represent three distinct artistic paths and perspectives, yet all share decades-long experience and professionalism.

Isabella Rossellini needs no introduction. Universally admired for her elegance and culture, she has often posed for the most renowned photographers and is an ideal host for the programme, capable of guiding the dynamic of the episodes with her refreshing, sincere curiosity.

Finally, we selected our twelve extraordinary contestants from among thousands of candidates, identifying the liveliest talents, the most original visions and the most courageous artistic choices. We can confidently avow that every photograph taken by the contestants on *Master of Photography* transmits a sense of the work, urgency and vision behind it, which is what gave us the idea for this unique photographic exhibition.

My thanks go to all the people who worked so enthusiastically in the Sky Arts Production Hub production unit and to Filippo Maggia, curator of the exhibition, who together made this project into a reality.

With the work carried out over these last few months and years by Sky Arte, but also by the entire Sky platform that has supported us all along, we hope to have demonstrated that television can and must be a powerful means of spreading culture.

Roberto Pisoni
Director Sky Arte HD

The exhibition and catalogue of the first *Master of Photography* series present the works of twelve photographers selected from those across Europe who responded to the call launched by Sky Arte HD (Italy, United Kingdom, Ireland, Germany and Austria) last autumn.

First, it should be clarified that, while *Master of Photography* is obviously conditioned by the competitive aspect, it distinguishes itself from the many programmes in the world of "talent shows", of which, admittedly, it is part.

First of all, participants were selected by a group of international experts. On the basis of their experience, these museum directors, critics and gallery owners evaluated a number of portfolios and rewarded those who expressed a genuine need to create images, as opposed to simply reproducing well-worn stereotypes.

The construction of each episode is also unique. The images, though adapted for the particular demands of television, are based on the original and founding genres of the discipline that are introduced, in fact, with masterpieces from the history of photography. These genres – portraits, nudes, landscapes and street photography – are essential for anyone serious about cameras, whether analogue or digital. In some cases, they have been elaborated in more challenging forms, such as the nightscapes that evolved out of street photography.

Finally, decisions about the resulting photographs were entrusted to a jury that boasted a visionary of the language of images, an experimental artist and devoted teacher of that language, and an exceptional professional portraitist. In this way, *Master of Photography* made it clear that the project is conceived not just as a competition where the best contestant wins, but as a training ground for new talent. What counts is participating and persevering as long as possible, even suffering in the process, all the while taking on new challenges in order to improve oneself and one's ability to reflect the world.

As the scientific consultant for the programme, I have observed a sort of genuine and, in certain ways, timid approach in all the photographers who, after successfully making it through the initial phase in which they explicitly sought to satisfy the tastes of the jury members, then understood that even more than their photos, they themselves were on the line. In this, they were undoubtedly supported by the valuable advice proffered by the teachers encountered in the various episodes.

The language of images predominates in today's world, to the point of prevailing over the language of words. It has thereby assumed an enormous responsibility, thanks also to the immediacy and ease with which it is transmitted and recognized. This is why *Master of Photography*, oriented as it is towards a mass public, is an appropriate means for enlightened viewing.

Filippo Maggia

Filippo Maggia is the Director and Head of Projects of Fondazione Fotografia Modena, photography curator at Fondazione Sandretto Re Rebaudengo in Turin, and photography editor for Skira.

CONTENTS

JUDGING PANEL

Rut Blees Luxemburg

is a German artist who creates large-scale photographic works, public art installations and opera stage sets representing the ever-changing urban landscape. Among her most celebrated works are *Piccadilly's Peccadilloes*, commissioned by Art on the Underground at London's Heathrow airport, and *Silver Forest*, a photographic monument in the heart of the Victoria district in London, as well as the iconic cover of the album *Original Pirate Material* by the rap group The Streets. She currently teaches in the Photography Department at the prestigious Royal College of Art, where she is also a reader in Urban Aesthetics. She has held exhibitions throughout the United Kingdom and Europe; one of the most remarkable was her solo show *Phantom*, a photographic exploration of the effects of modern architecture on Dakar, Senegal, which opened at the Tate Liverpool in 2003. Her work can be seen in public institutions including the Tate Modern, V&A Museum, and the Centre Georges Pompidou.

Simon Frederick

was born in London of Caribbean parents
from the island of Grenada. Being self-taught,
Simon was never conditioned by the
conventions that academic studies, tradition
or even technique sometimes impose.
At the heart of his work is a passion for
people and their cultures, which inspires
his visual exploration of the many varied
expressions of human nature. Thanks to his
fame as a photographer, he had the chance
to branch out into many fields, from celebrity
portraits and art exhibitions to global
advertising campaigns. His transition to film
director came quite naturally, as he directed
musical promos that are in fact short films,
documentaries and, more recently,
advertisements. As a director, he is esteemed
for his unusual talent for creating exciting,
engaging work with a unique visual style.
This year Simon Frederick is taking on new
challenges, writing his first full-length feature
film and preparing his most ambitious project
– a major portrait exhibition accompanied
by a documentary and limited edition book,
all scheduled for Fall 2016.

Oliviero Toscani

is world-famous as the creative force behind
some of the most well-known and original
brands ever. Over the years, he has created
corporate images and advertising campaigns
for Esprit, Chanel, Fiorucci, Prénatal, and
many other labels, while as a fashion
photographer he has contributed to
international magazines including *Elle, Vogue,
GQ, Harper's Bazaar, Esquire, Stern, Libération*,
and many others. Between 1982 and 2000,
he created the image, identity, communication
strategy and online presence of United Colors
of Benetton, transforming it into one of
the most immediately recognizable, widely
known brands in the world. In 1990, he
designed *COLORS*, the first global magazine,
and in 1993 he conceived and directed
Fabrica, an international centre for research
in the arts and modern communication.
He has been awarded many prizes, including
four Golden Lions at the Cannes Lions
Festival, the UNESCO Grand Prize, two
Grand Prix de l'Affichage, and numerous
prizes from Art Directors Clubs in cities
such as New York, Tokyo, Berlin and Milan.

PHOTOGRAPHERS

Dragica Carlin
Croatia / England, 44 years old

Born in Croatia, Dragica Carlin lives and works in London. Although she is a painter, she uses photography in her creative process to help express moods and sensations, to capture the energy of the city, and to tell stories of daily life. Often her work immortalizes objects or situations that underline the precariousness of life, invisible or hidden spaces. "I try to understand the existence of the things around me, why they exist and how they exist", she explained. Dragica observes situations, people and their thoughts in the context of their lives, which leads her to explore the relationship between the metaphysical and material worlds, between man and his surroundings.

Rupert Frere

England, 35 years old

Rupert lives and works in London. After entering the army, he served as a photographer in the British Army, assigned to Afghanistan a full three times. Emotion is the principal element in his photographic practice, in which he seeks daring, unusual perspectives to convey the point of view of soldiers on their mission, thus sharing intimately with them the places and events underway. He loves to photograph people since he believes that they are by far the most intriguing subject. Although he is accustomed to working in dangerous, emergency situations, the last time he was truly afraid was when, having been invited to do a portrait of Her Highness Queen Elizabeth II, she politely communicated that the photograph was too dark. Impassioned and tough, yet still with a great sense of humour, Rupert sees *Master of Photography* as a chance to show the world what he is capable of when "armed" with a camera.

Neal Gruer

Scotland, 30 years old

Neal, who is half Scottish and half Ghanese, became a photography enthusiast at the age of eighteen. Although he studied law and worked as a lawyer in London, he renounced his legal career and returned to Glasgow to devote himself full-time to art. Still, he does not like to call himself an "artist", though he considers himself a creative person, and while he plays the violin, reviews films and is writing a novel, photography remains his greatest love. He generally shoots digital but is also fascinated by the analogue process. His work grows out of an intense study of his subjects; never stopping at the surface, Neal delves deep to reveal the origins and history of the people he encounters, seeking to highlight traits shared by everyone, independent of their particular culture.

Marta Lallana García

Spain, 21 years old

Marta was born in Spain in 1994. After
attending art school in Zaragoza, she fell in
love with photography while studying cinema
at the Universitat Pompeu Fabra in Barcelona.
Though she usually works in digital, she
is fascinated with film and its delayed
gratification, as well as the opportunity to
capture moments that can never be repeated.
Her images are shot in a natural, spontaneous
style, often portraying people in the midst
of their daily activities, which explains why
she prefers to edit as little as possible.
As she considers herself a neophyte, she
views *Master of Photography* as a welcome
challenge where she can demonstrate
her passion for this discipline by taking
the best possible images while also growing
through an exchange of ideas with other
photographers.

Gabriele Micalizzi

Italy, 31 years old

Gabriele is convinced that art is the only real proof of man's evolution. Formerly a soccer player and tattoo artist from Milan, he has been working as a professional photojournalist for the past ten years. According to Gabriele, history and its cyclic repetition are a necessary point of reference, parameters in which communications and the press play such a crucial role today. Over the years, he has often exhibited his images taken in the field. While he prefers digital, he is also interested in analogue and loves black and white for its iconographic power and dramatic immediacy. Gabriele is particularly drawn to political and social issues, often operating in war zones in North Africa and the Middle East as an envoy for several international newspapers. It is his belief that photography has the power – and the duty – to raise questions; to this end, his images often appear like short stories revealing the emotions of his subjects, men and women who are out of the spotlight and far from the media world.

Lanka Perren

France, 39 years old

Lanka was born in France in 1976 and graduated from the Conservatoire libre du cinéma français in Paris. Since 1999, he has divided his time between Ireland and France. He has worked on a variety of photographic and cinematic projects, won a number of awards, and participated in the production of four short films for *The Lives of Spaces* exhibition in the 11th Architecture Biennial in Venice. Although his passion for photography only developed recently, he has already evolved a personal style oriented towards photojournalism and publishing. He loves the creative energy of photography and seeks to transform it into a visual experience in every image. Lanka prefers working in digital because he wants to see the result immediately and loves natural light, even though he finds it more difficult to control. All in all, he considers photography a way to explore reality and leave his mark on it.

Yan Revazov
Russia, 35 years old

Yan Revazov was born in the Black Sea
region, Russia, in 1980. Although he studied
at the Bolshoi Ballet Academy in Moscow and
became a professional dancer, he discovered
a passion for photography at the age of
nine, when he found a Zorki in his house and
proceeded to transform his bedroom into
a full-fledged dark room. Throughout his
career as a dancer, he shot photos during
performances, on stage, and backstage. When
an accident forced him to give up dancing,
however, he turned to photography full-time,
and today it means everything to him.
He worked for several theatres and companies
before moving to Berlin, where he has
a studio. He loves theatre photography,
especially shooting portraits of artists
that reveal their inner nature.

Sebastian Siebel

Germany, 42 years old

Sebastian is a professional photographer
and light technician living in Berlin.
He pursued his passion for photography,
which developed during his school years,
into a full-time career in the discipline.
Over the years, he has worked with Peter
Lindbergh, Ralph Mecke, Mario Testino,
David Bellemere, Glen Luchford, Annie
Leibovitz and Martin Schoeller. In his photos,
he tries to offer his personal vision of reality
and uncover secrets concealed within the
visible world. Eclectic, dynamic and broad-
minded, he views *Master of Photography*
as a stimulus for his creativity and a chance
to carry his photography to a higher level
in order to stage a major solo exhibition.

Gina Soden

England, 30 years old

Gina is a photographer living in London.
Central to her idea of photography is a desire
to explore the limits of beauty, decadence,
nostalgia and neglect through abandoned
sites and derelict buildings. Shunning a
documentary approach, however, she relies
on a vision that highlights composition, forms
and volumes in constant equilibrium. Each
image is the outcome of the superimposition
of two types of travel: physical travel, with
all the difficulty of gaining access to these
often hidden or even off-limits sites, and
temporal travel, which she invents by
transforming the real, tangible world into
a vision. Gina has exhibited in prestigious
national and international galleries and
obtained numerous prizes. Should she win
the *Master of Photography* competition,
she will have the chance to realize her
ambitious dream of travelling to the
furthest corners of the world.

Mary Stuart

Italy, 30 years old

For Mary Stuart, born and raised in Rome,
photography is a healing process, a form
of art therapy. She is solitary and taciturn
by nature, but when her mother gave her
a camera, Mary discovered that photography
could help her explore the world and
concretize her ideas through the lens; so
she quit law school to devote herself entirely
to this discipline. Since she prefers portraits
and night shots, she often works with a tripod
to allow for long exposure times. Her imagery
is inspired by the paintings of Edward Hopper,
depicting sombre, melancholic urban subjects
that make an immediate impact. Mary
considers herself very competitive and hopes
to face new challenges during *Master of
Photography*.

Hongwei Tang

Austria, 23 years old

Hongwei Tang is an amateur photographer
living in Vienna. As a youth, he began
expressing his creativity through the
production of light graffiti, setting down
the path of his future career. For Hongwei,
photography is a powerful means to express
oneself with perfect freedom, experimenting
conceptually and transforming abstract
ideas and visions into concrete reality.
He is particularly interested in travel and
socially committed photography; in both
cases, he aims to grasp the differences
and peculiarities that determine the
uniqueness of an individual's life. Photography
of architecture and street photography,
especially nightscapes, are likewise spheres
of interest. Hongwei considers himself
ambitious and curious, so with the *Master
of Photography*, he is eager to leave
the confines of his world and overcome
his personal limits.

Laura Zalenga

Germany, 26 years old

Laura, from southern Germany, studied
architecture in Munich but then decided
to become a freelance photographer.
Photography evolved into her greatest
passion because it allows her to tell stories
and communicate emotions. In fact, for Laura,
the best compliment is to hear that people
are moved by her photos. While she aims
to incorporate refugees and animal rights
activism into her photography, most of her
images are actually self-portraits because
she believes that spending time alone
provides an opportunity for self-discovery,
understanding and acceptance – in the end,
only those at peace with themselves can bring
peace to others. Highly demanding of herself
and never content with her work, Laura sees
Master of Photography as an excellent chance
to grow and learn.

THE BEAUTY
OF ROME

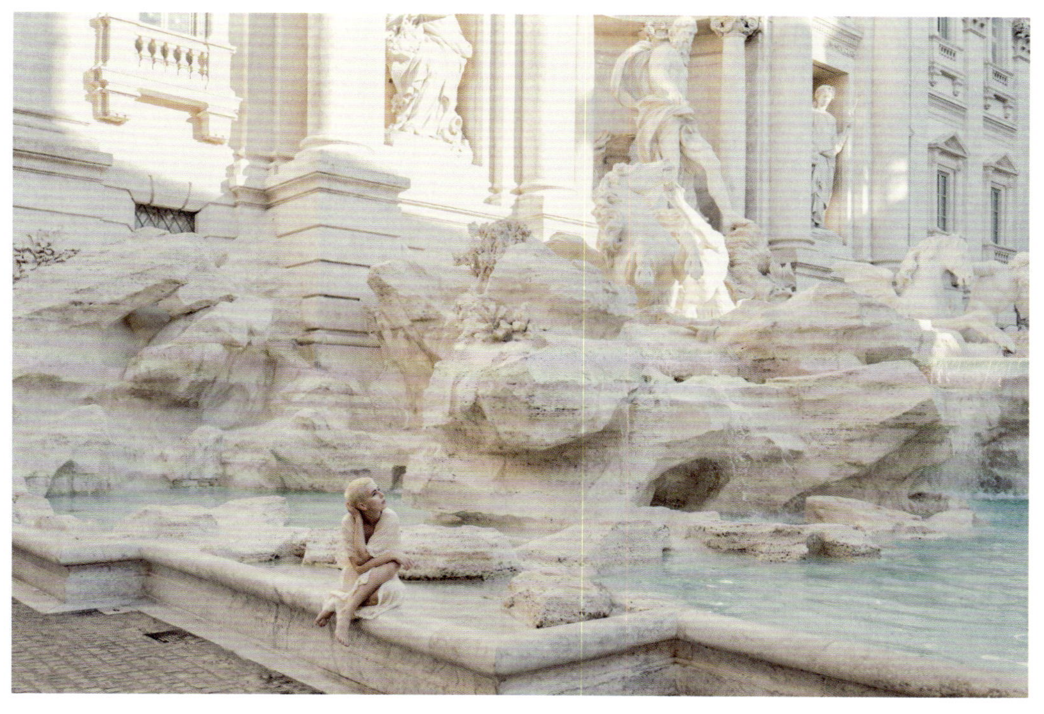

Laura Zalenga

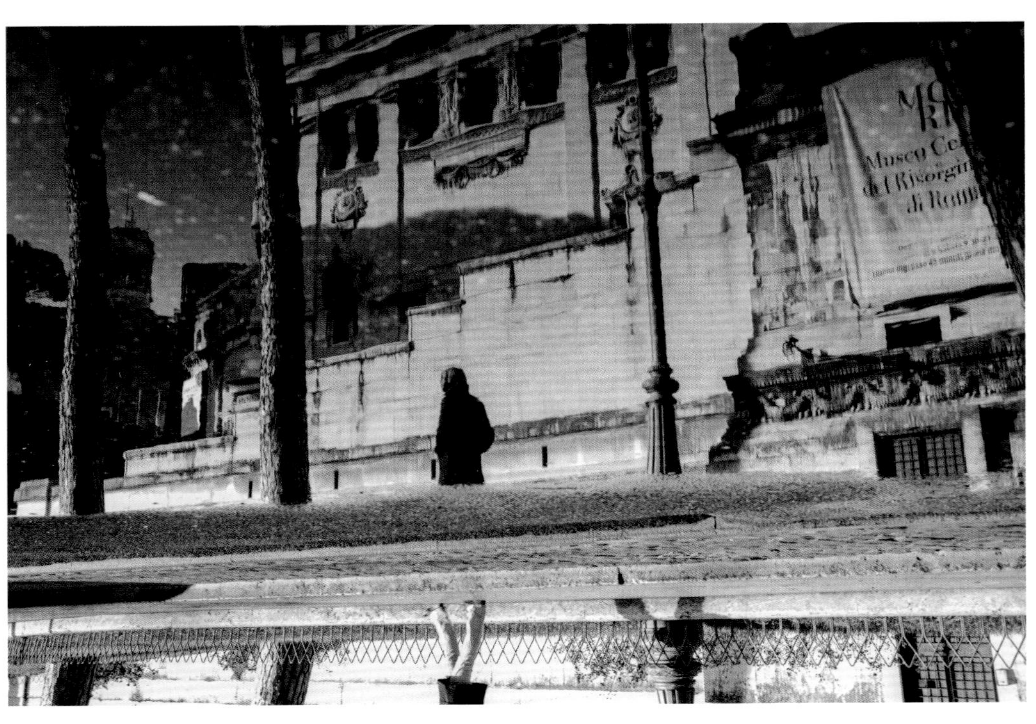
MU
RI
Musco Ce
del Risorgi
di Rom

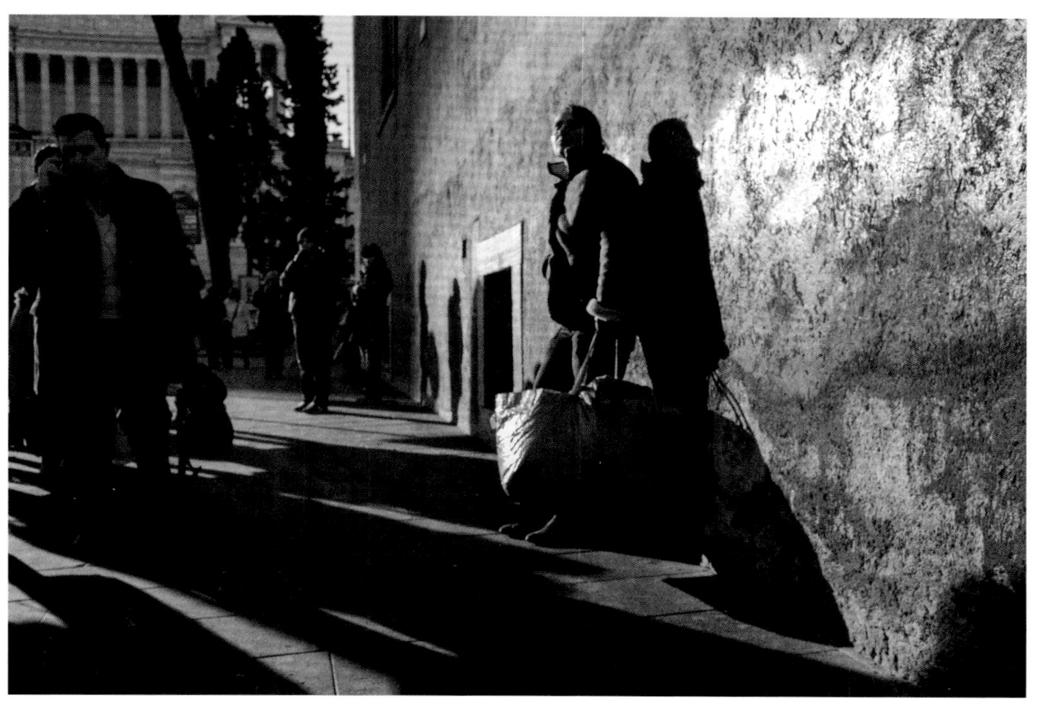

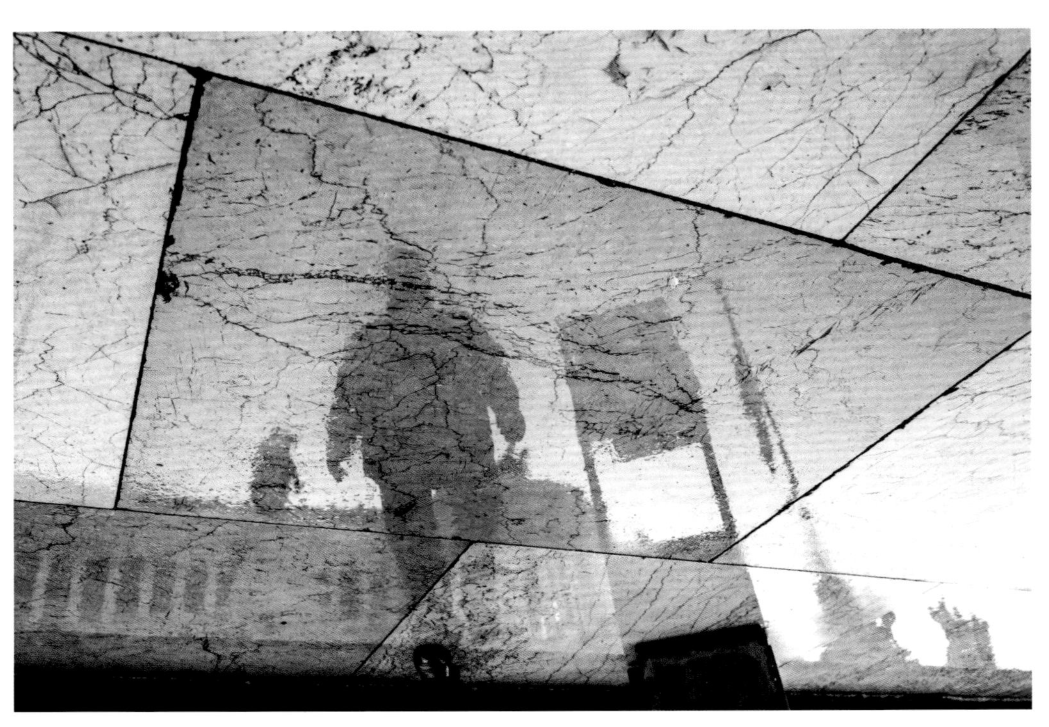

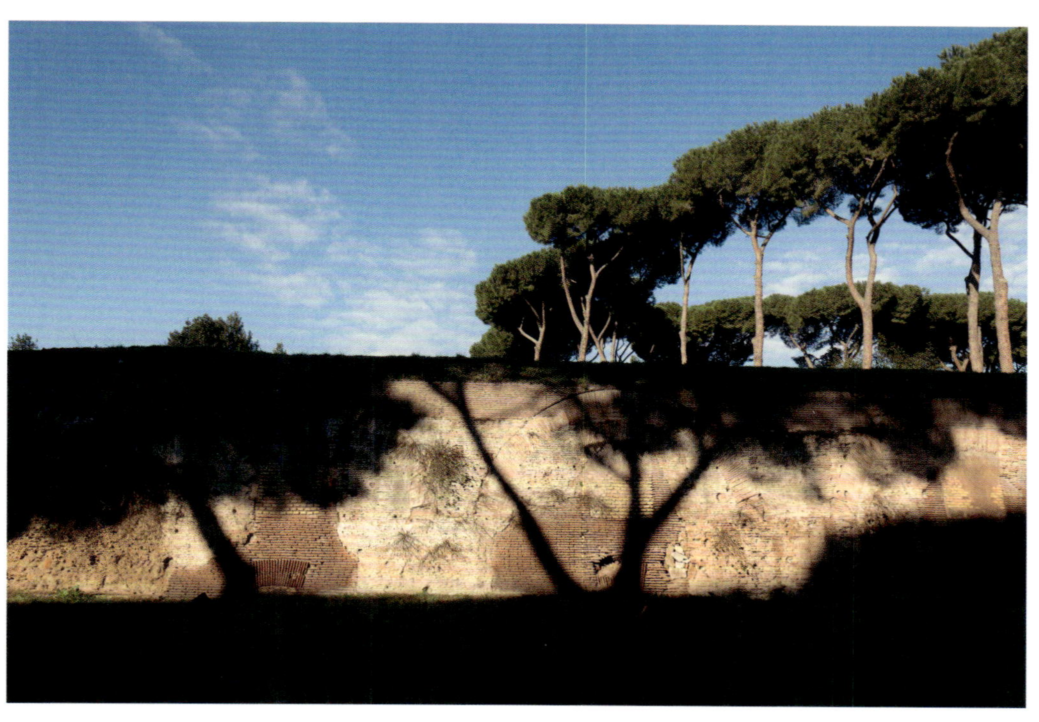

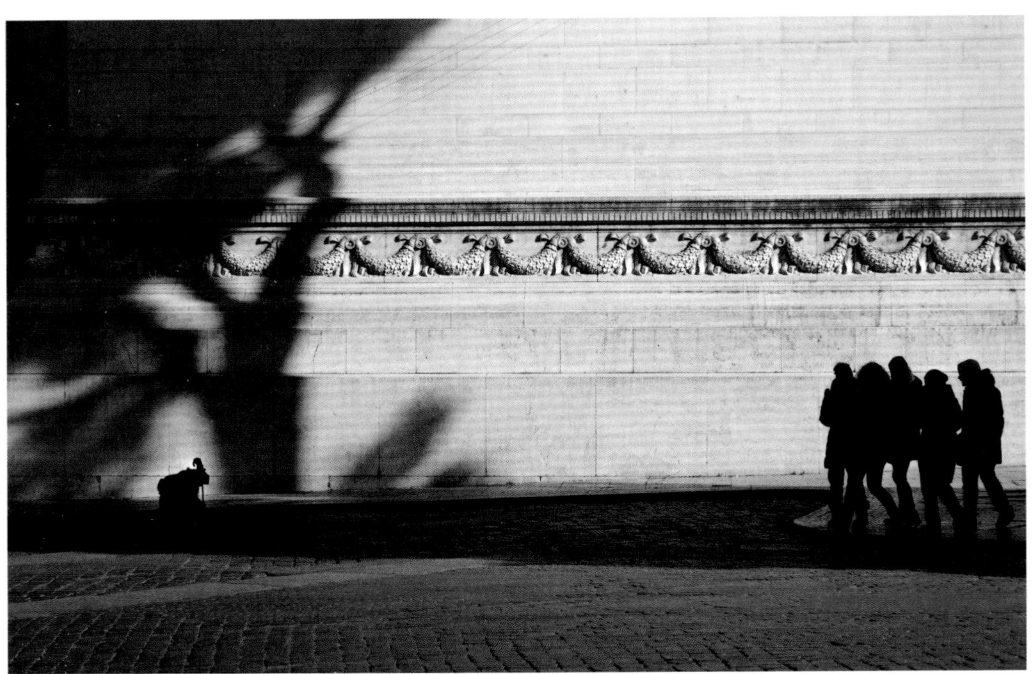

Marta Lallana García

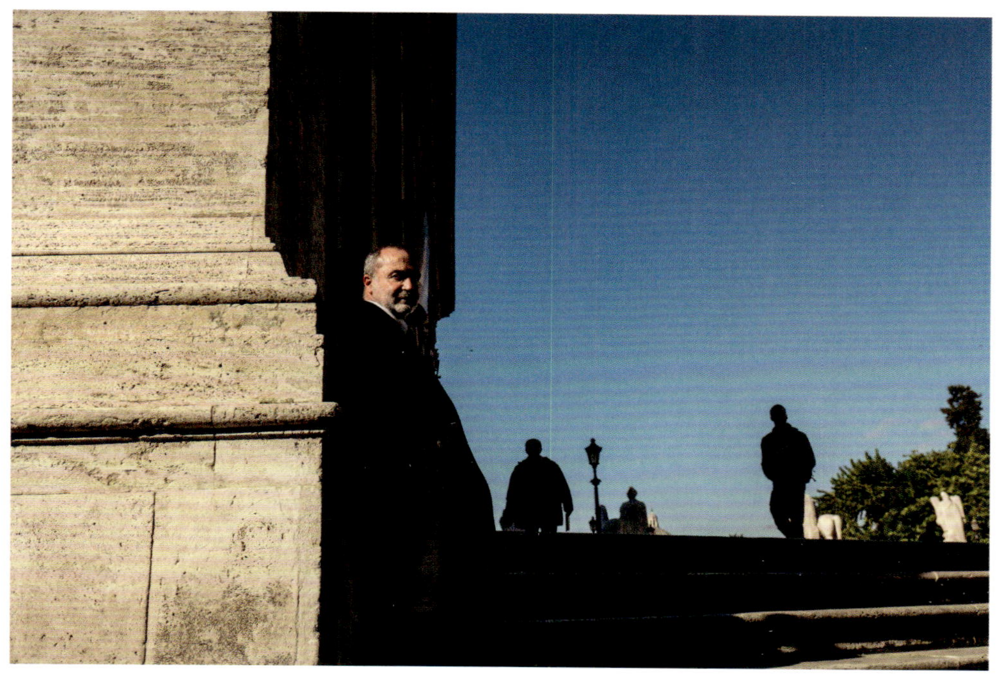

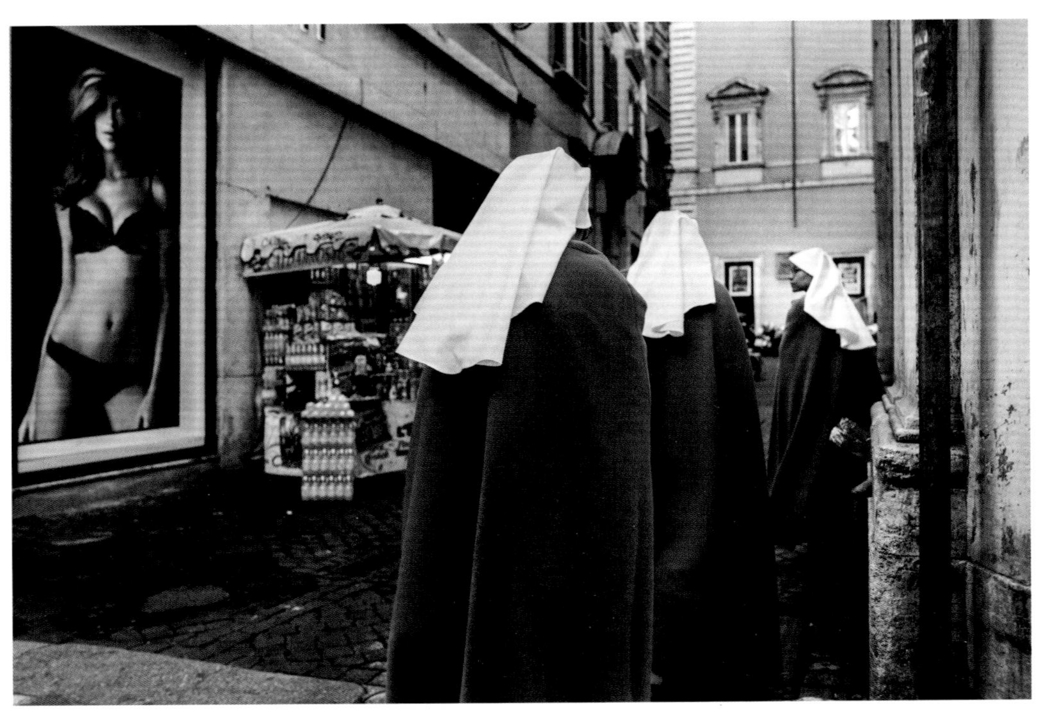

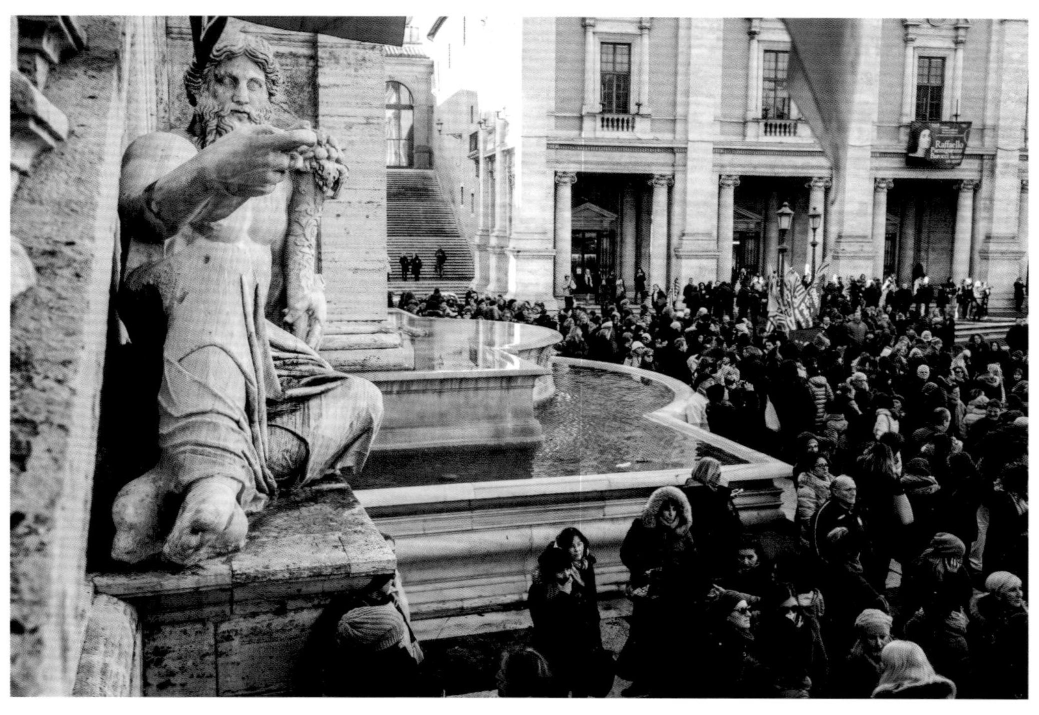

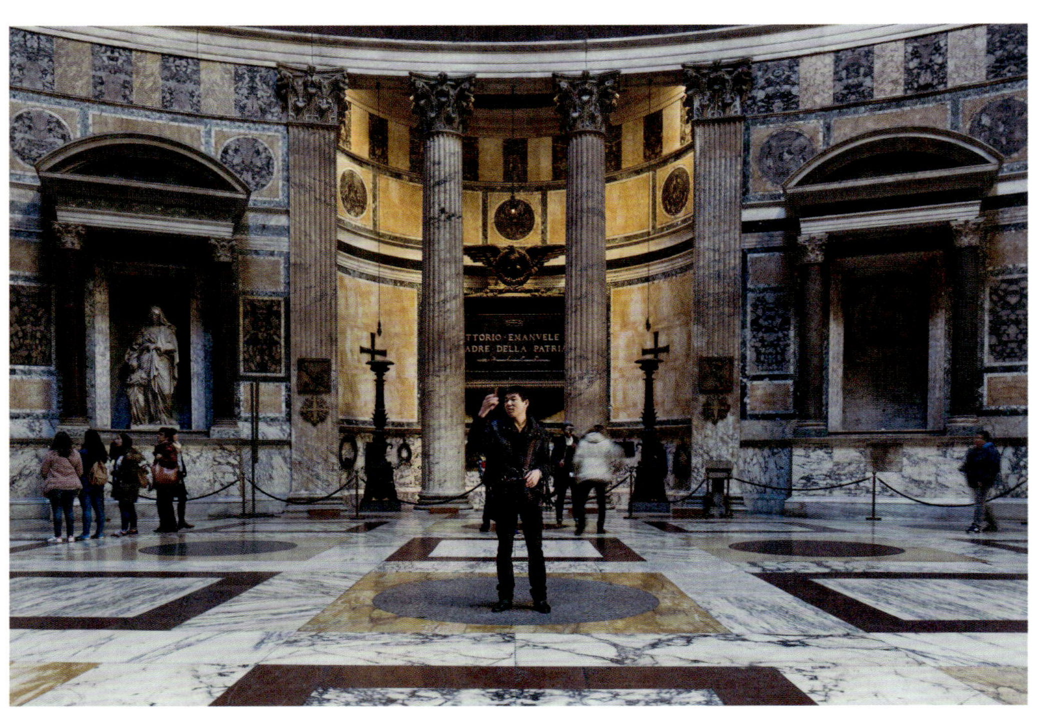

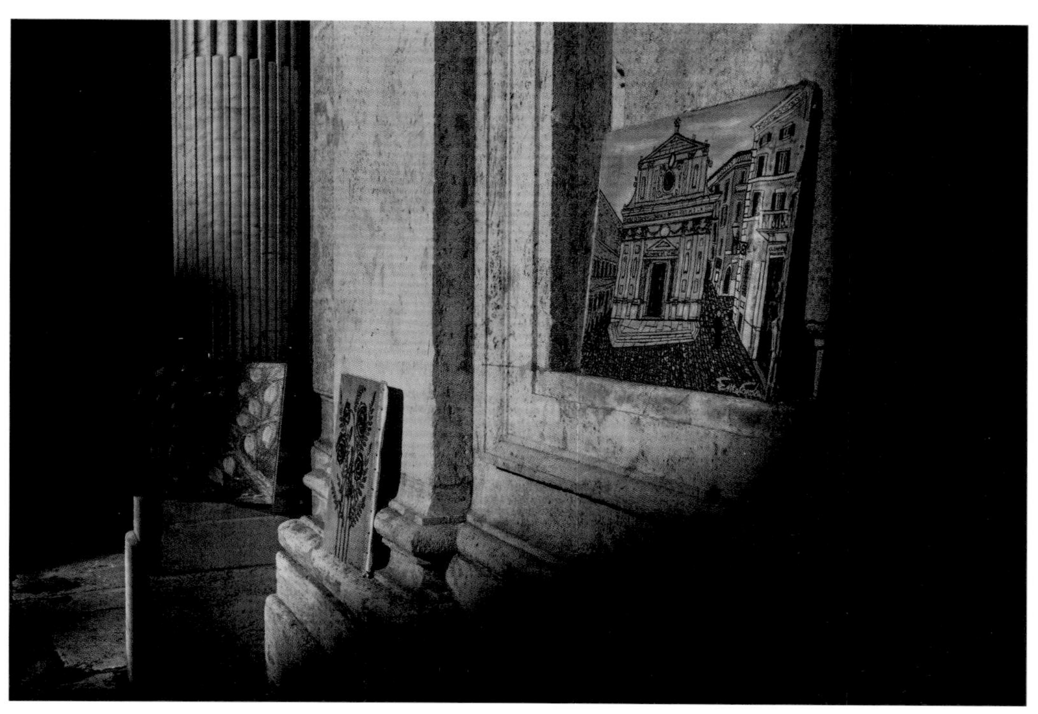

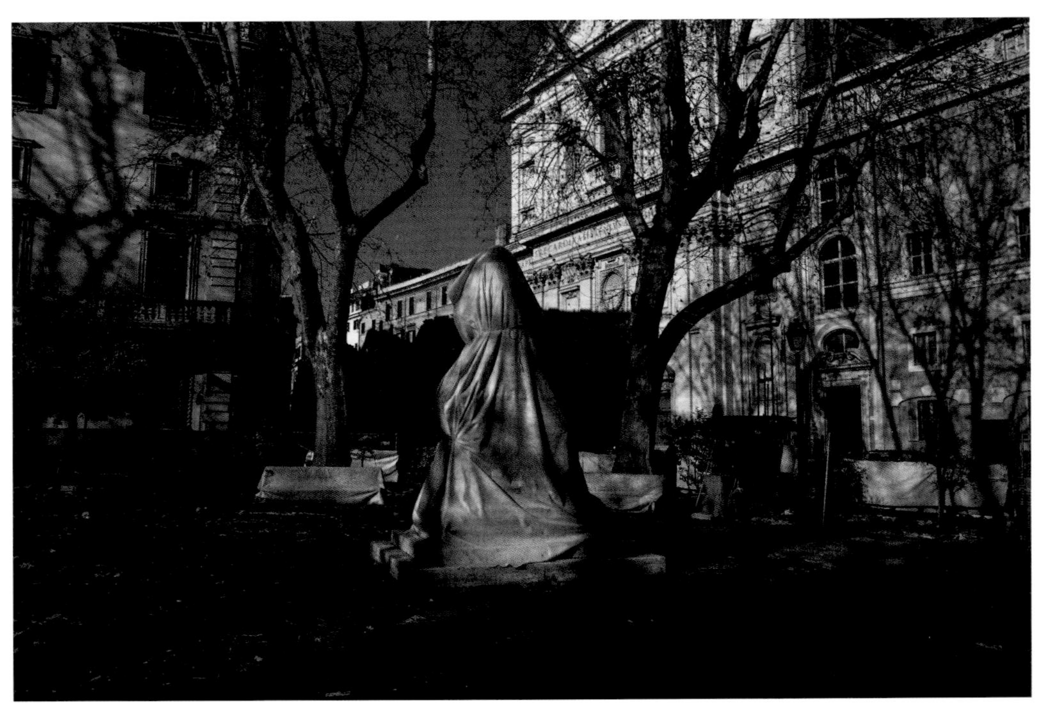

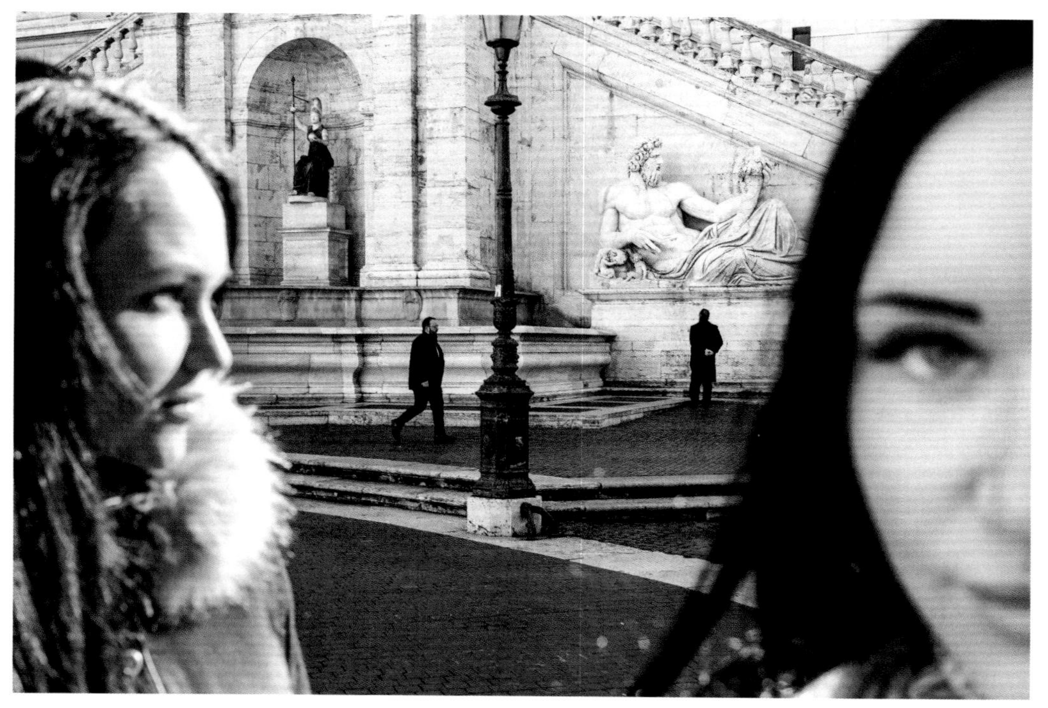

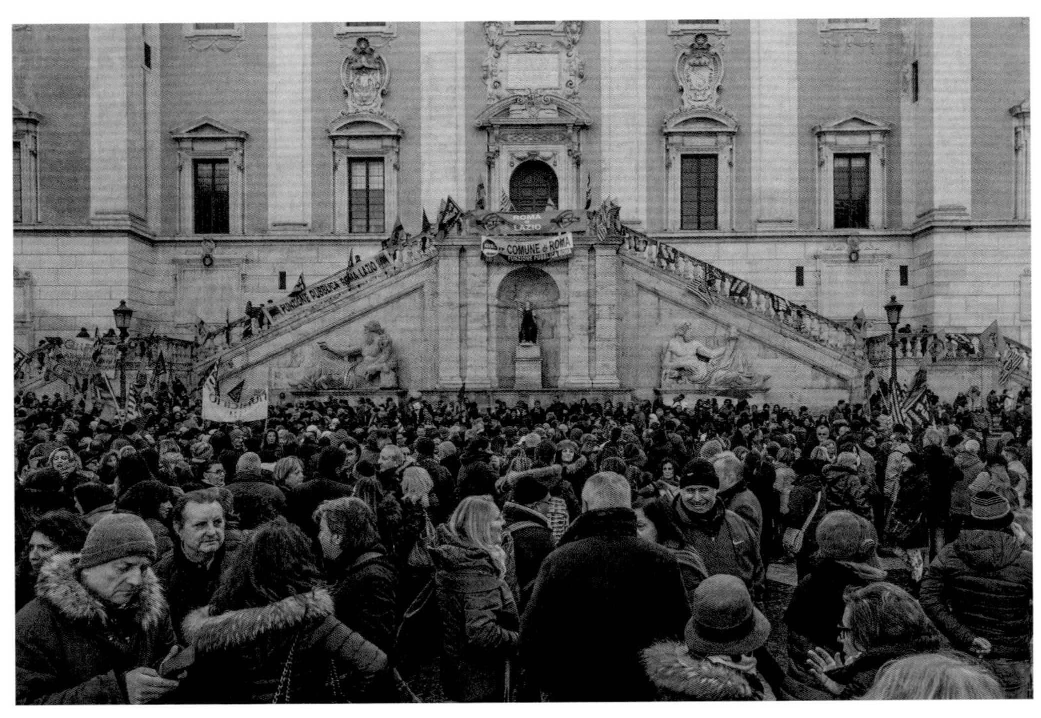

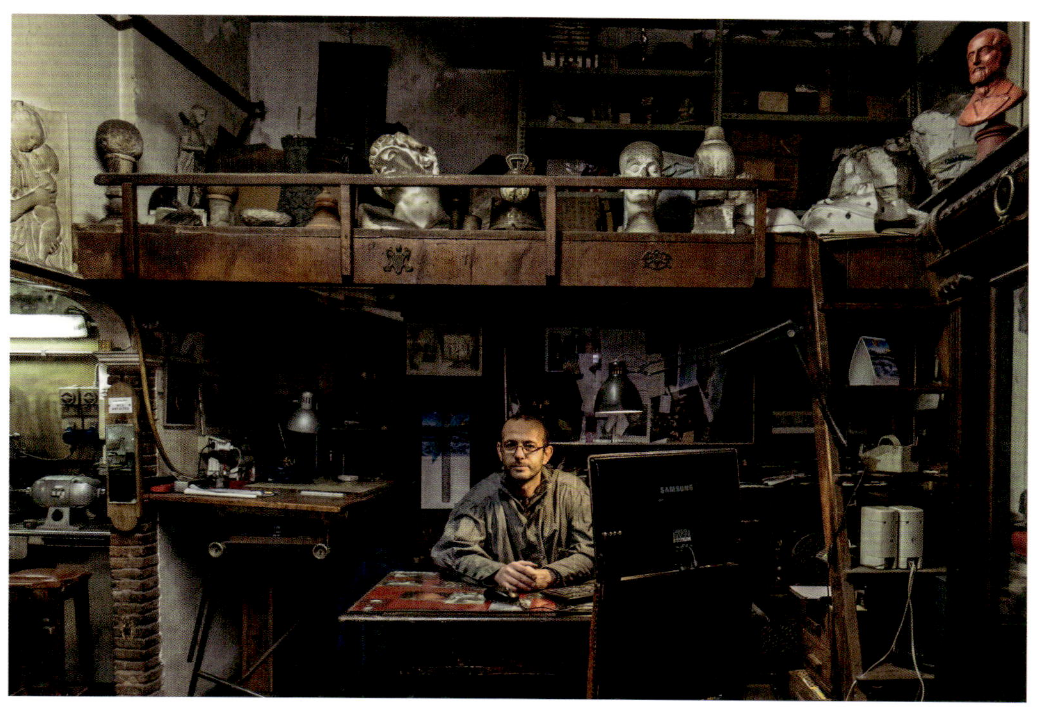

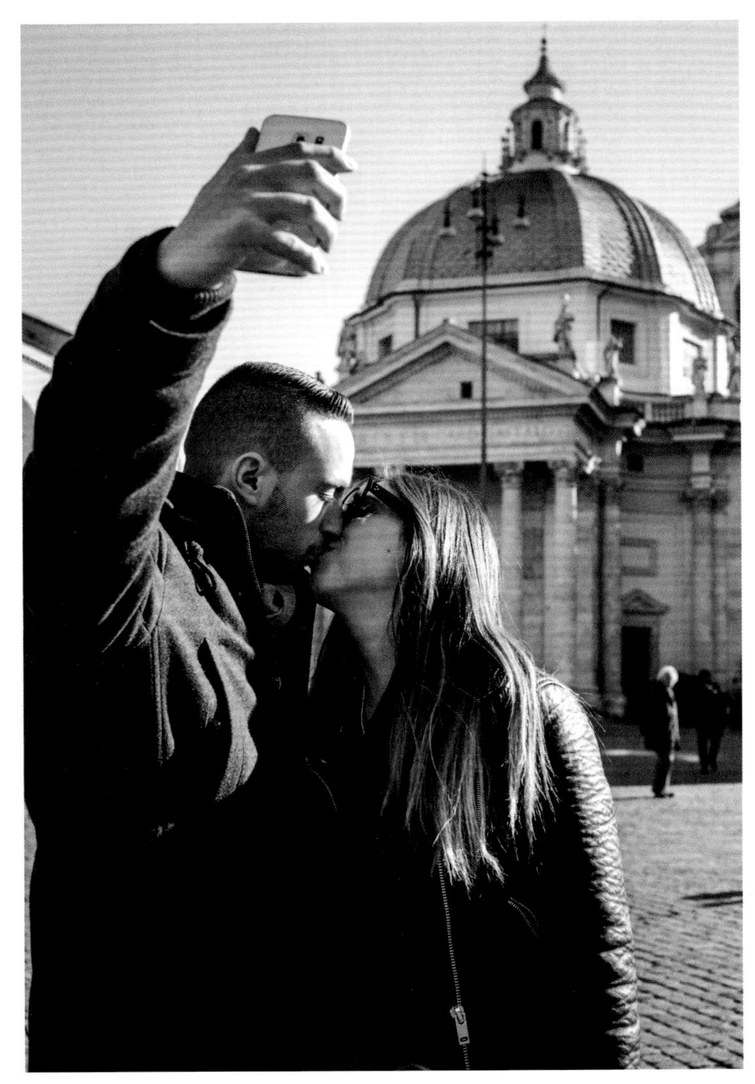

Rupert Frere

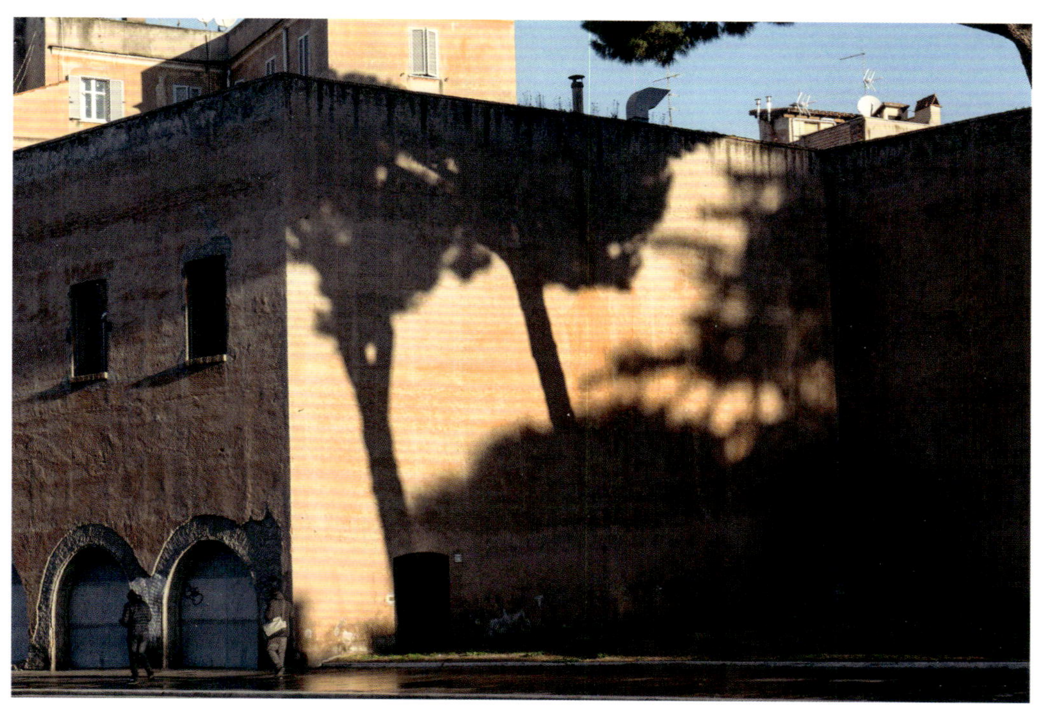

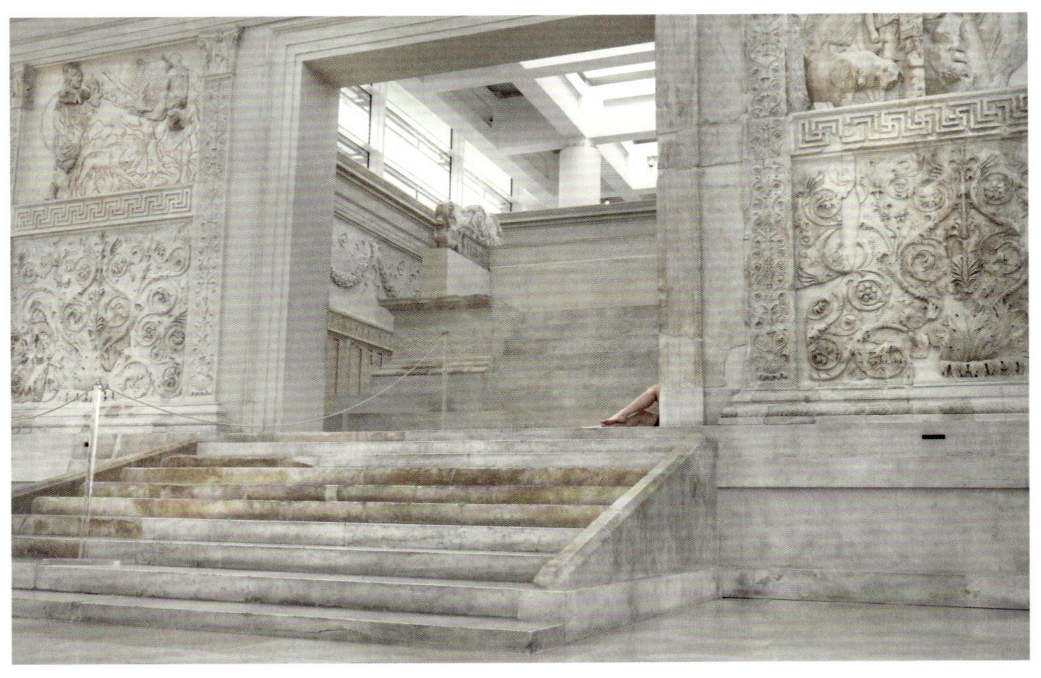

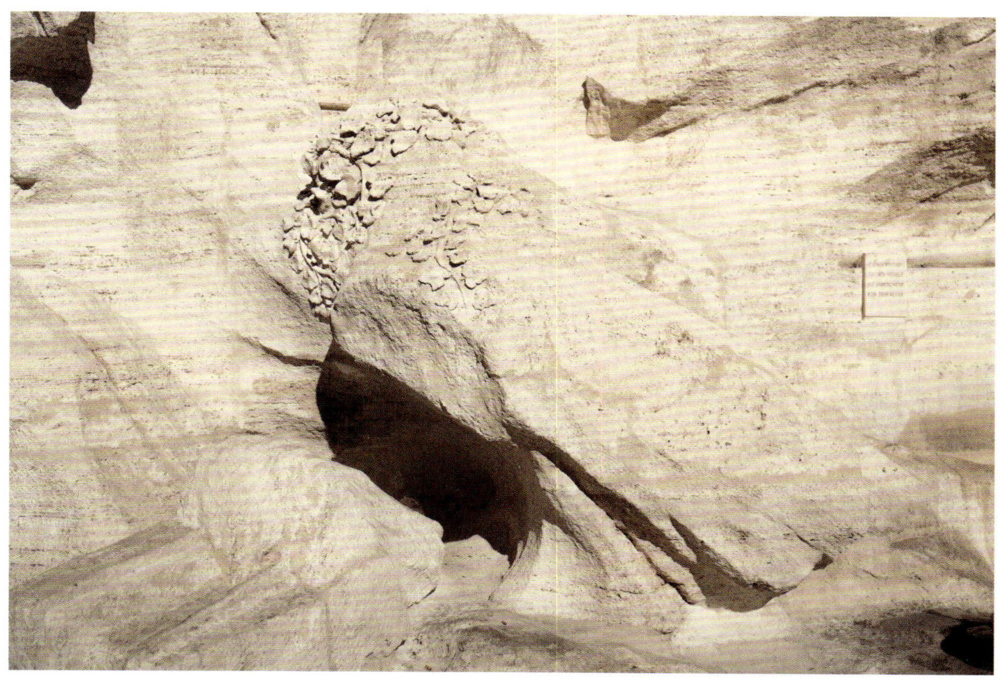

Dragica Carlin

BERLIN NIGHTLIFE

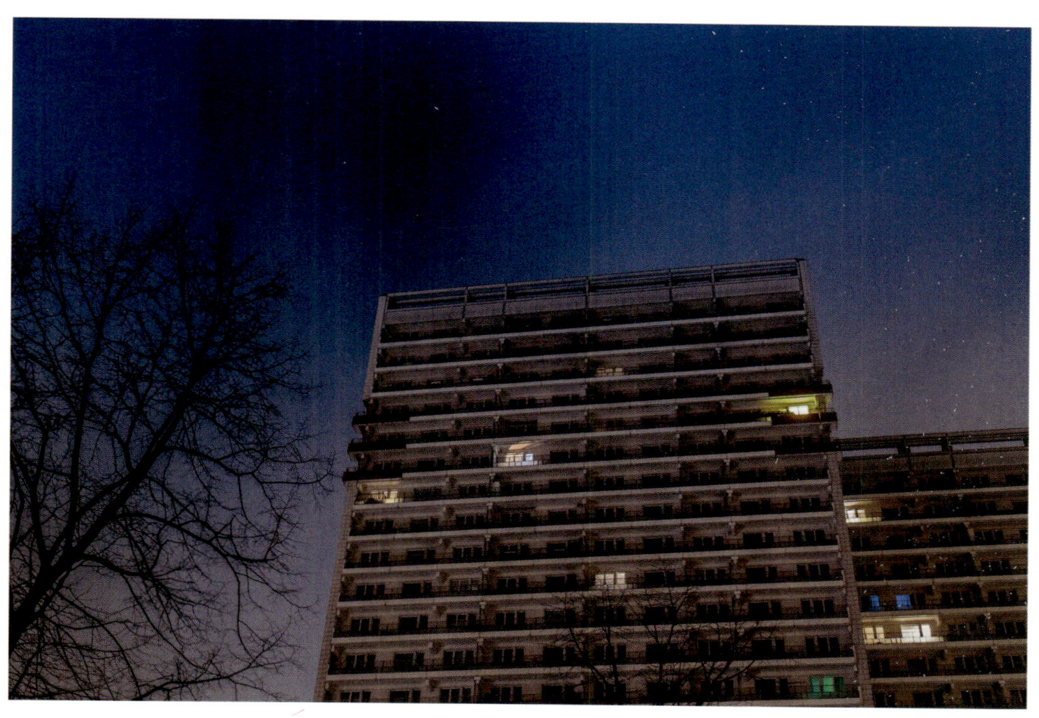

Marta Lallana García

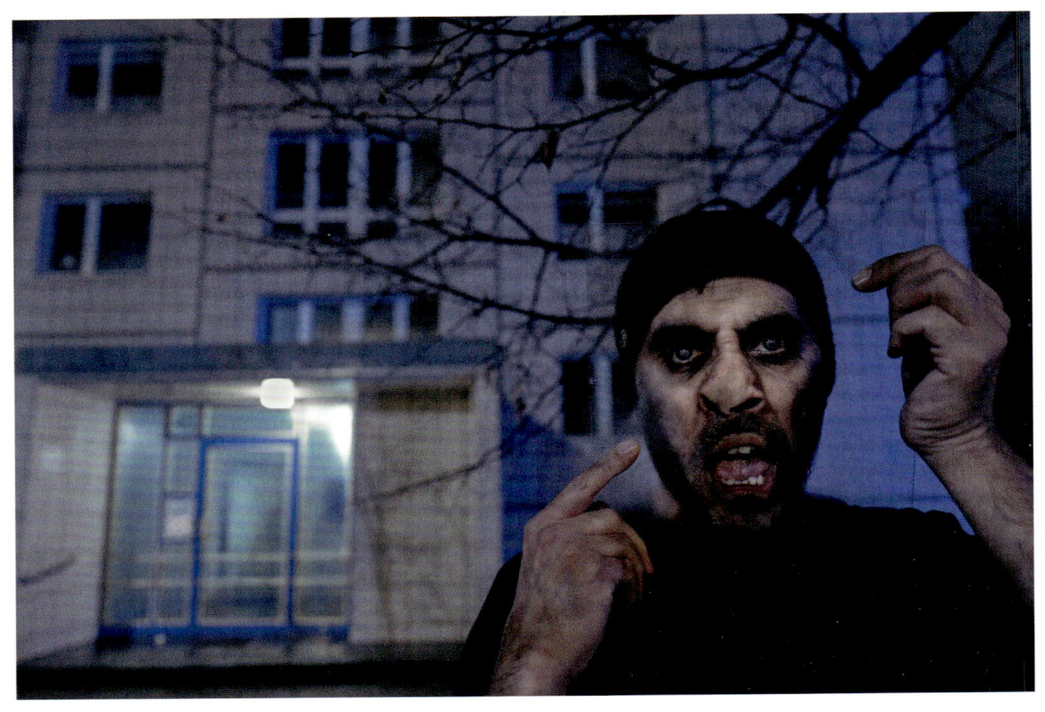

Marta Lallana García

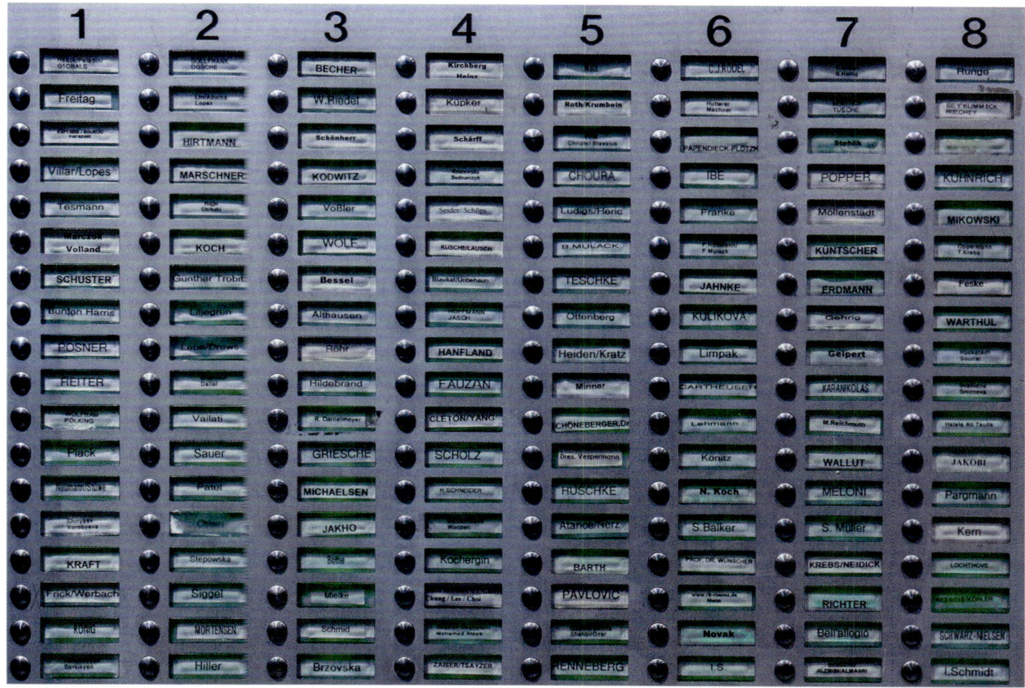

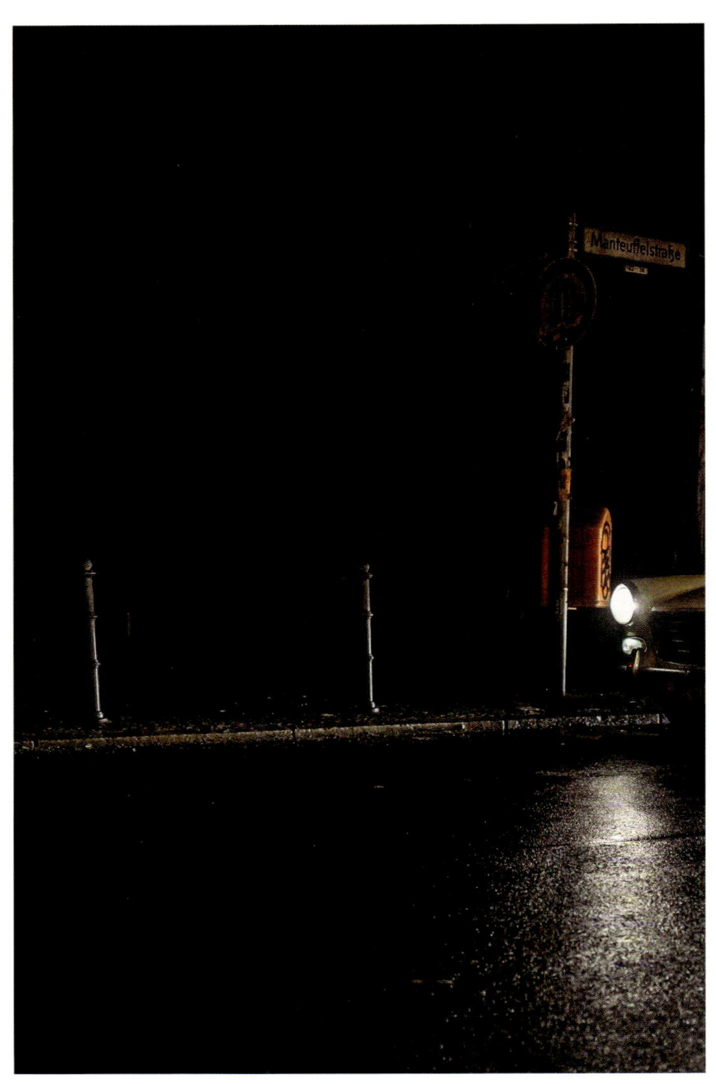
Manteuffelstraße

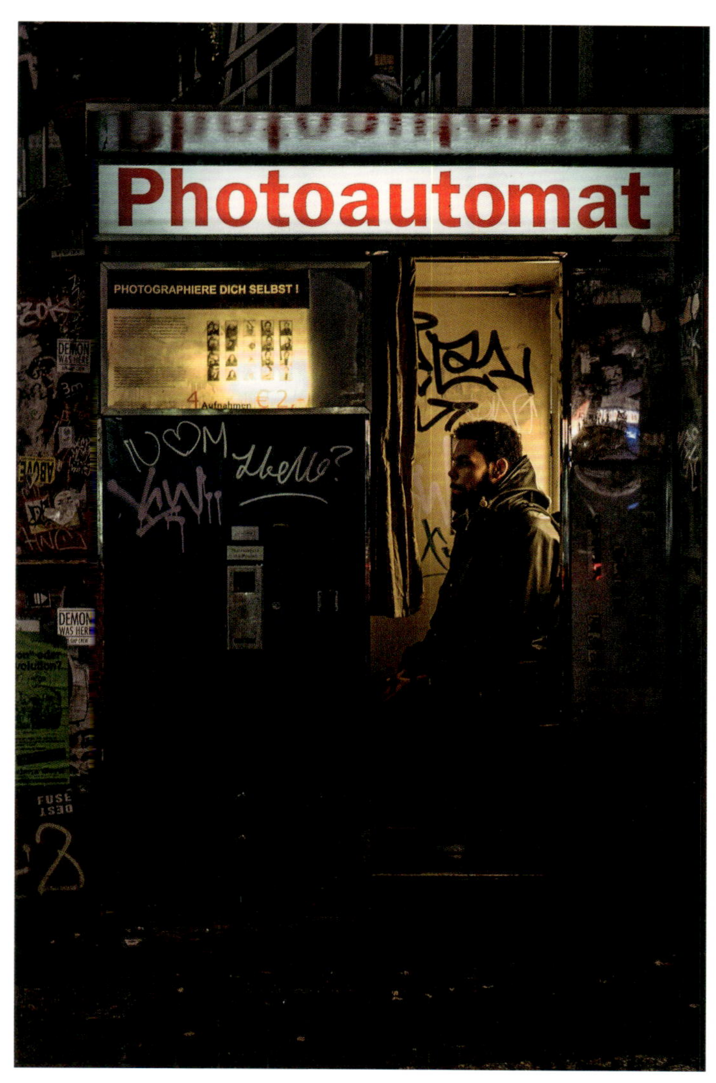

Photoautomat
PHOTOGRAPHIERE DICH SELBST !
4 Aufnahmen €2
DEMON WAS HERE
FUSE DEST

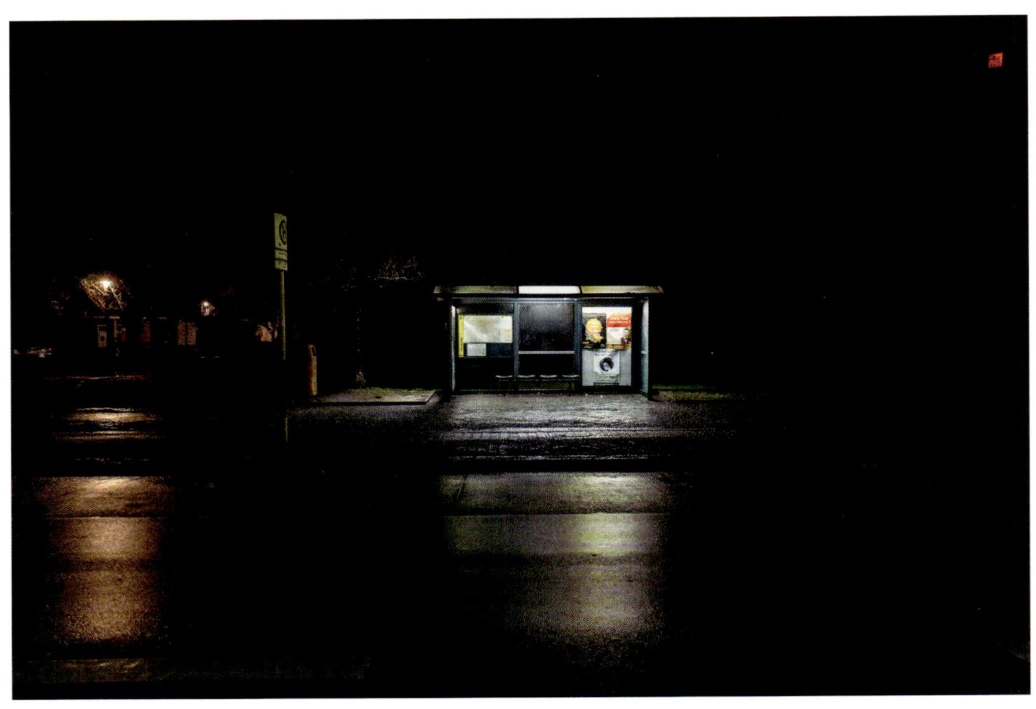

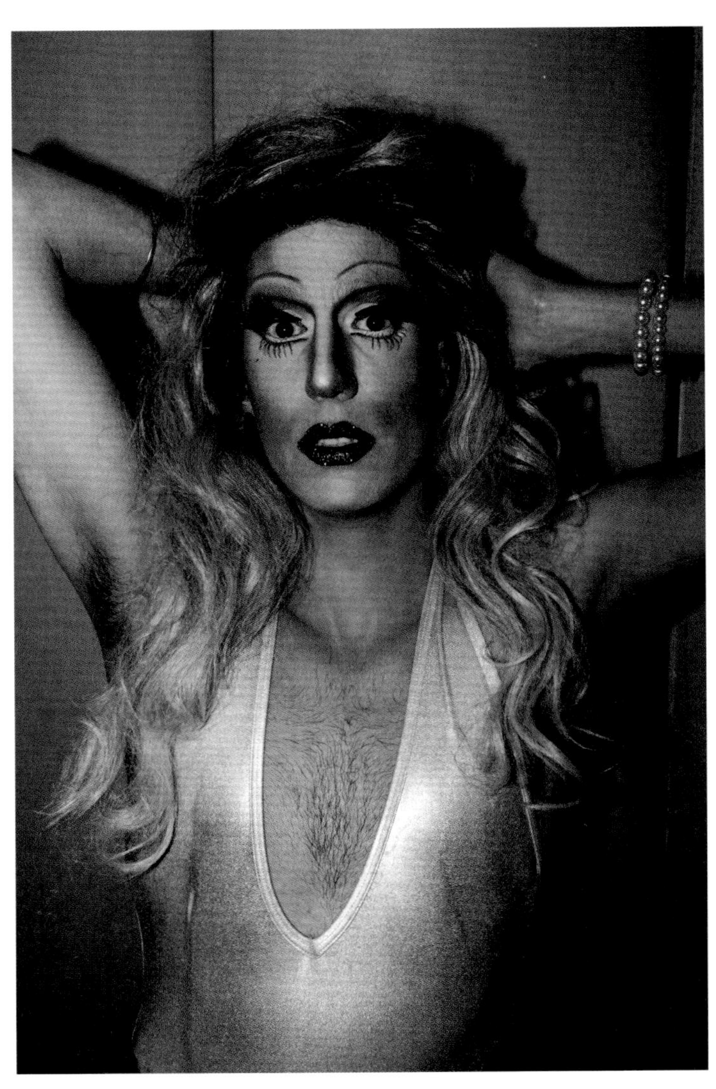

Mary Stuart

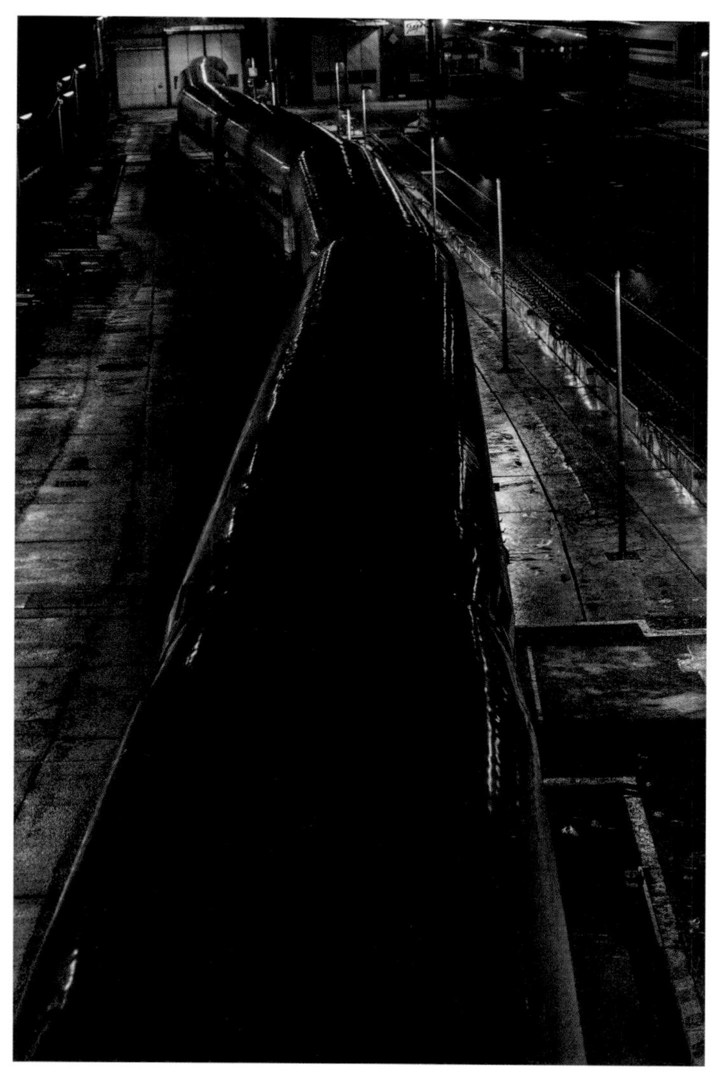

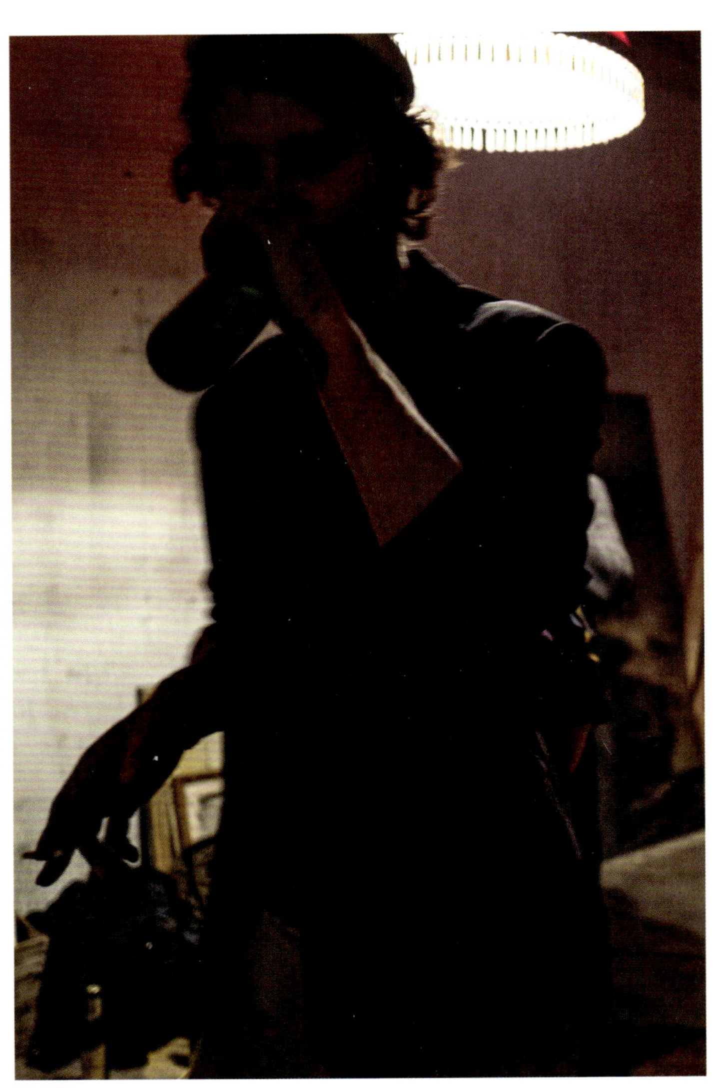

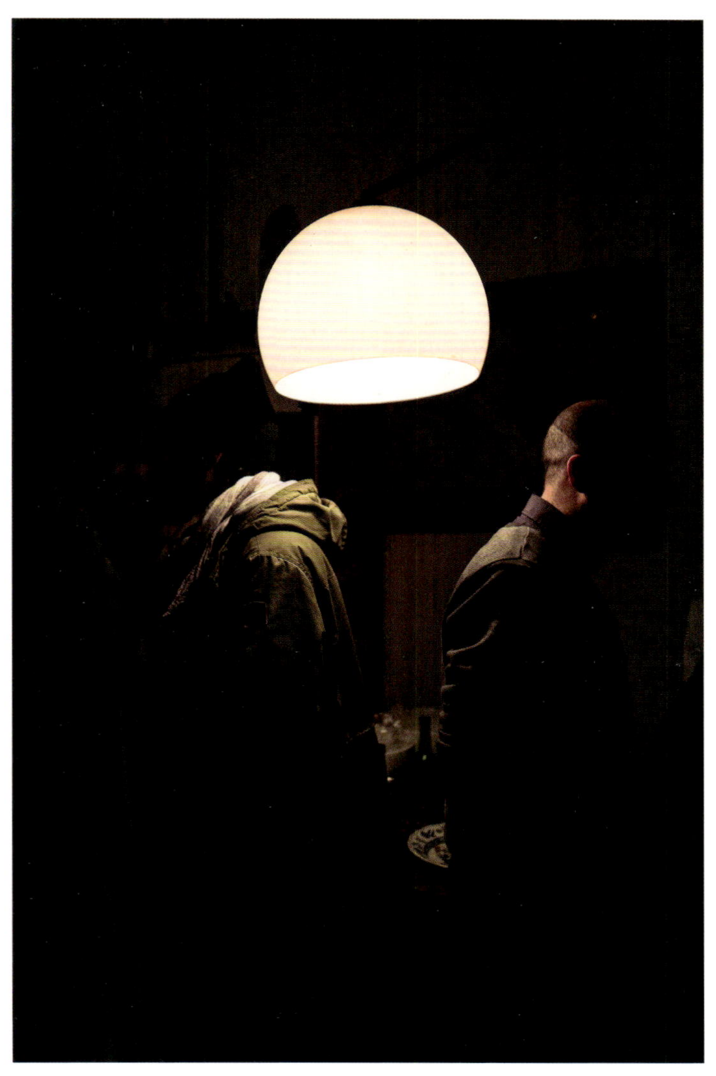

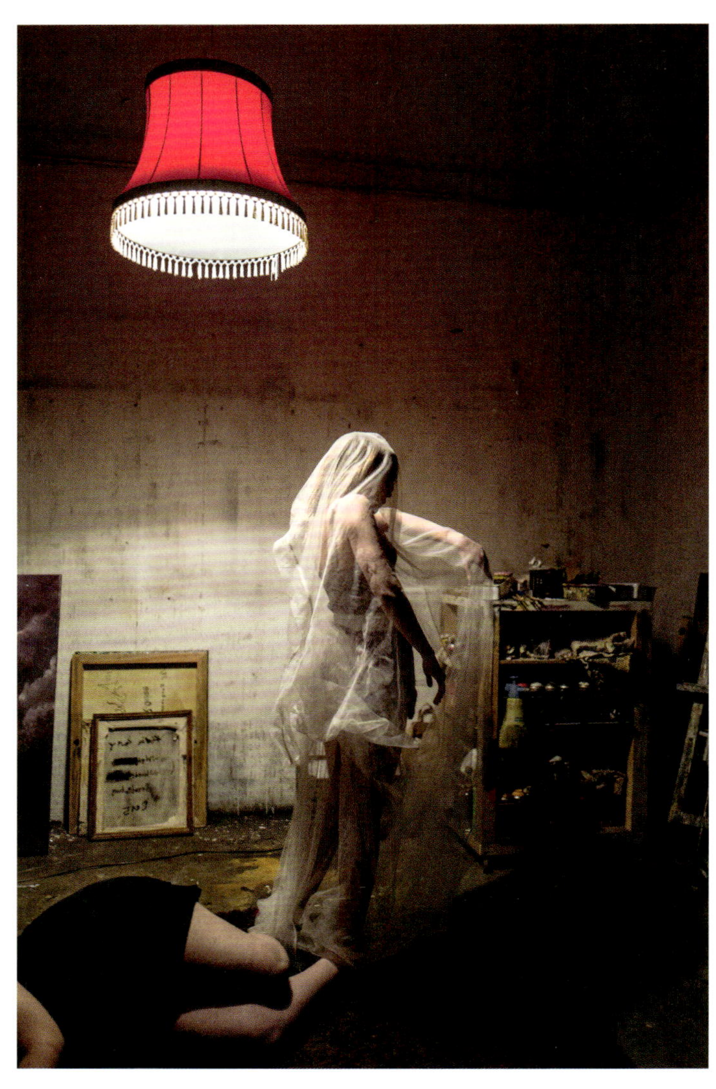

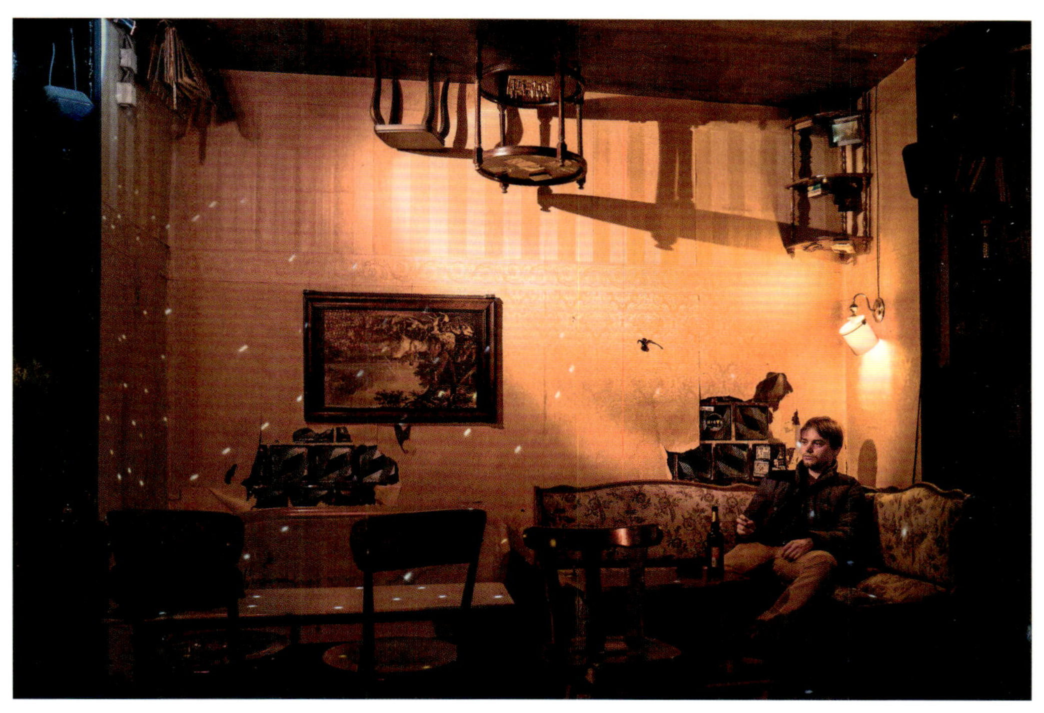

Rupert Frere

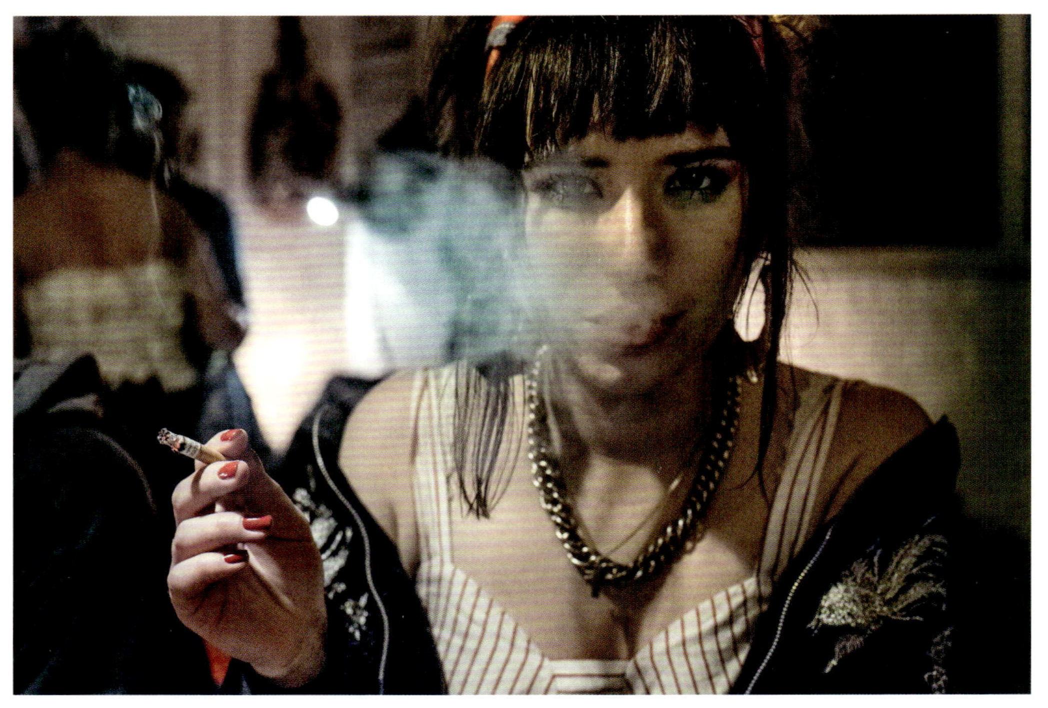

Rupert Frere

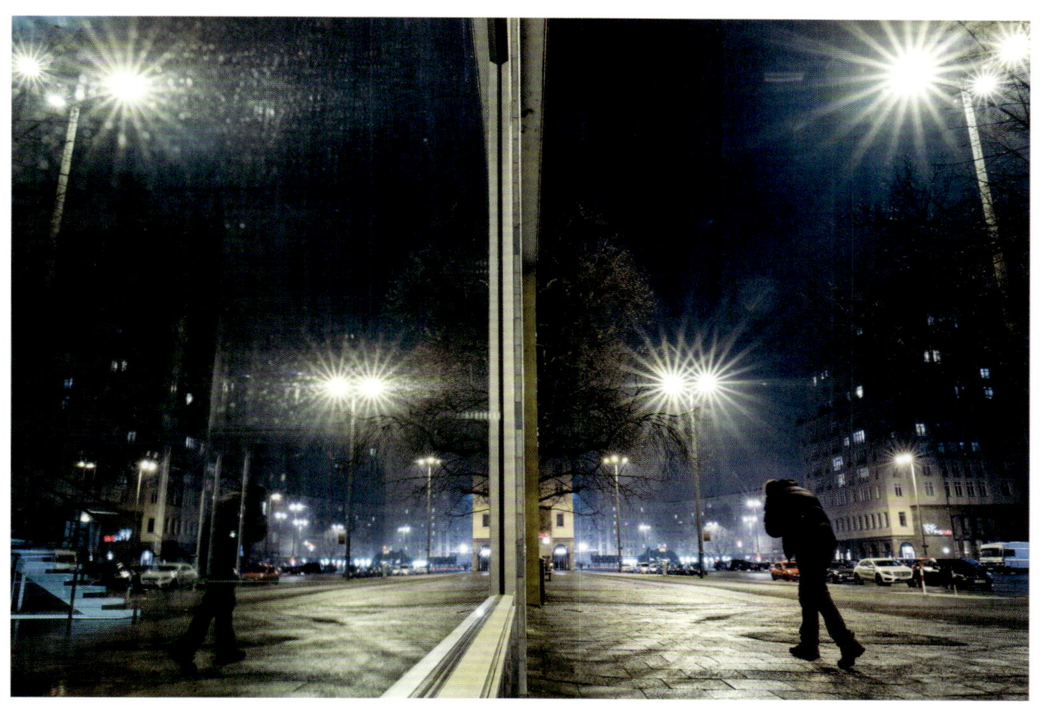

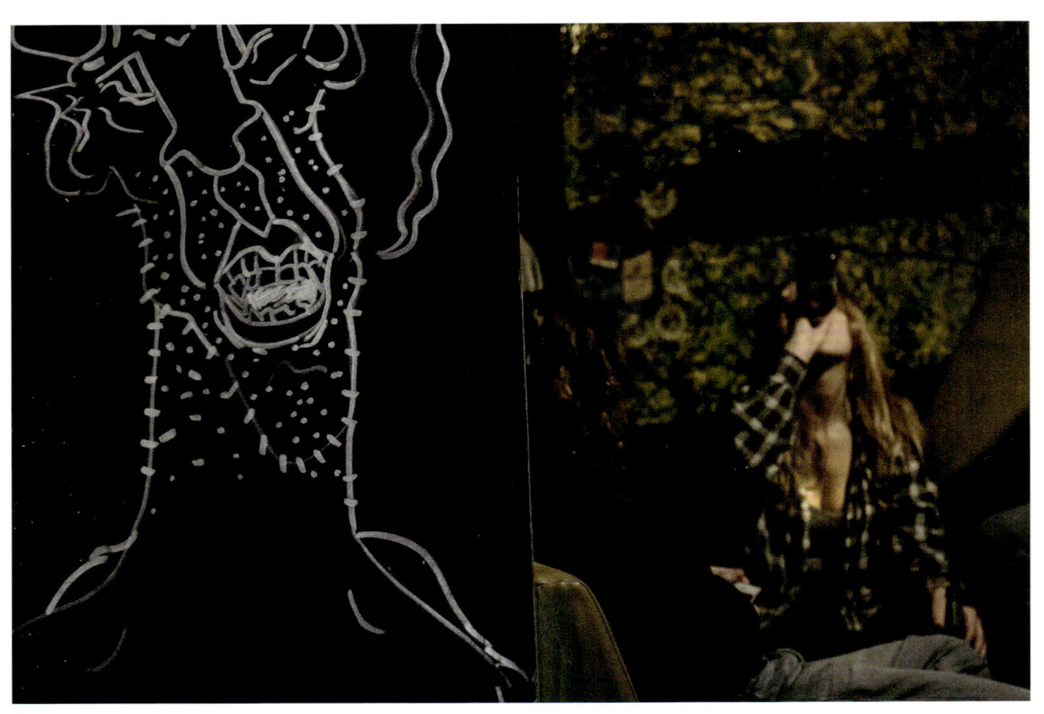

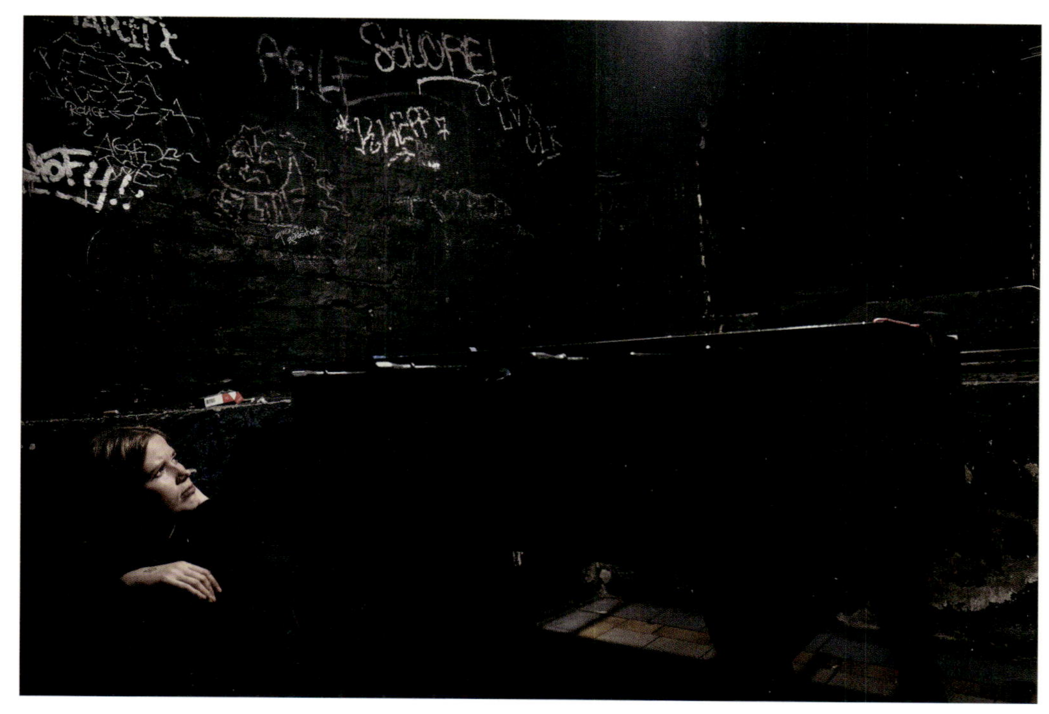

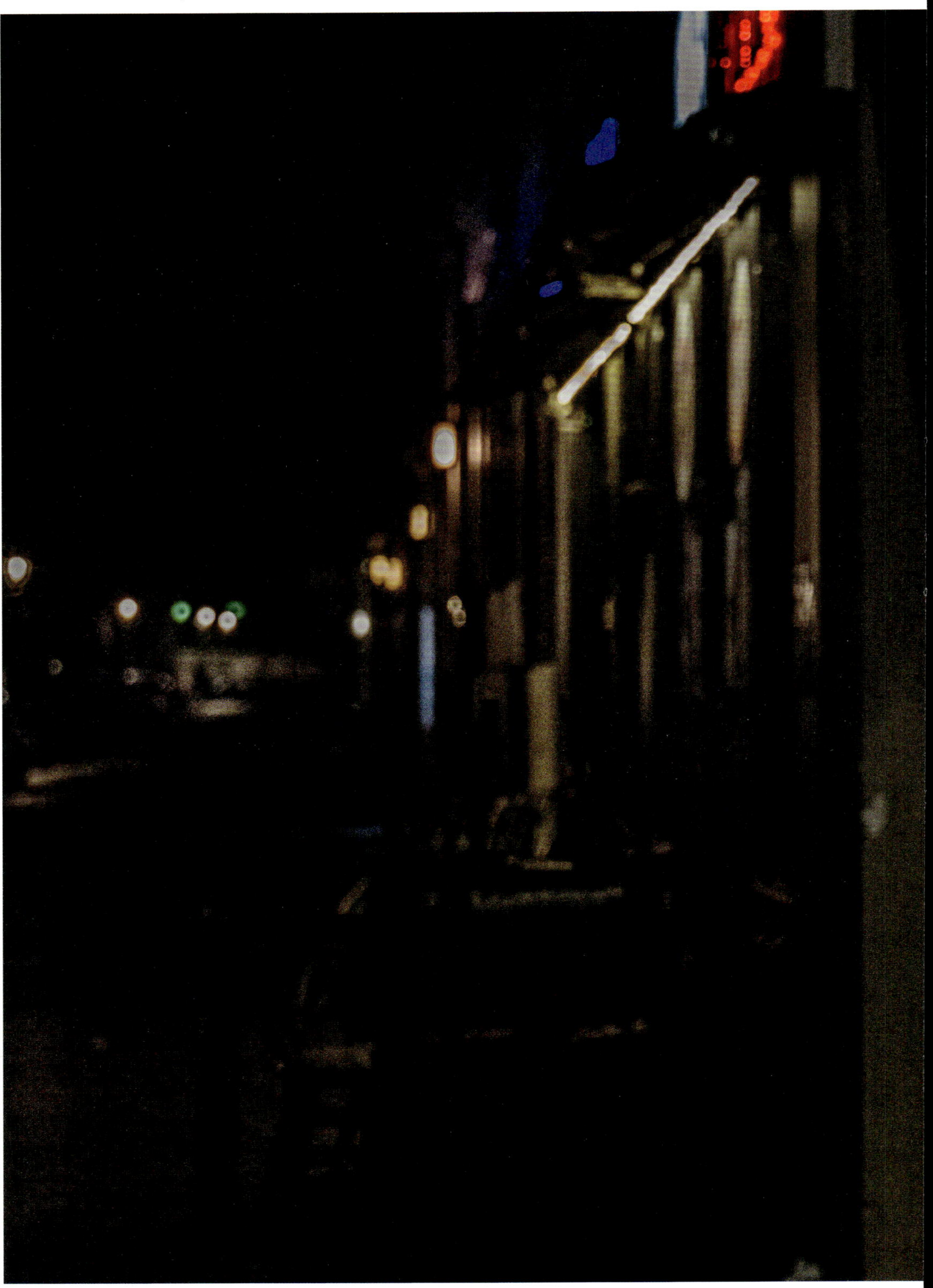

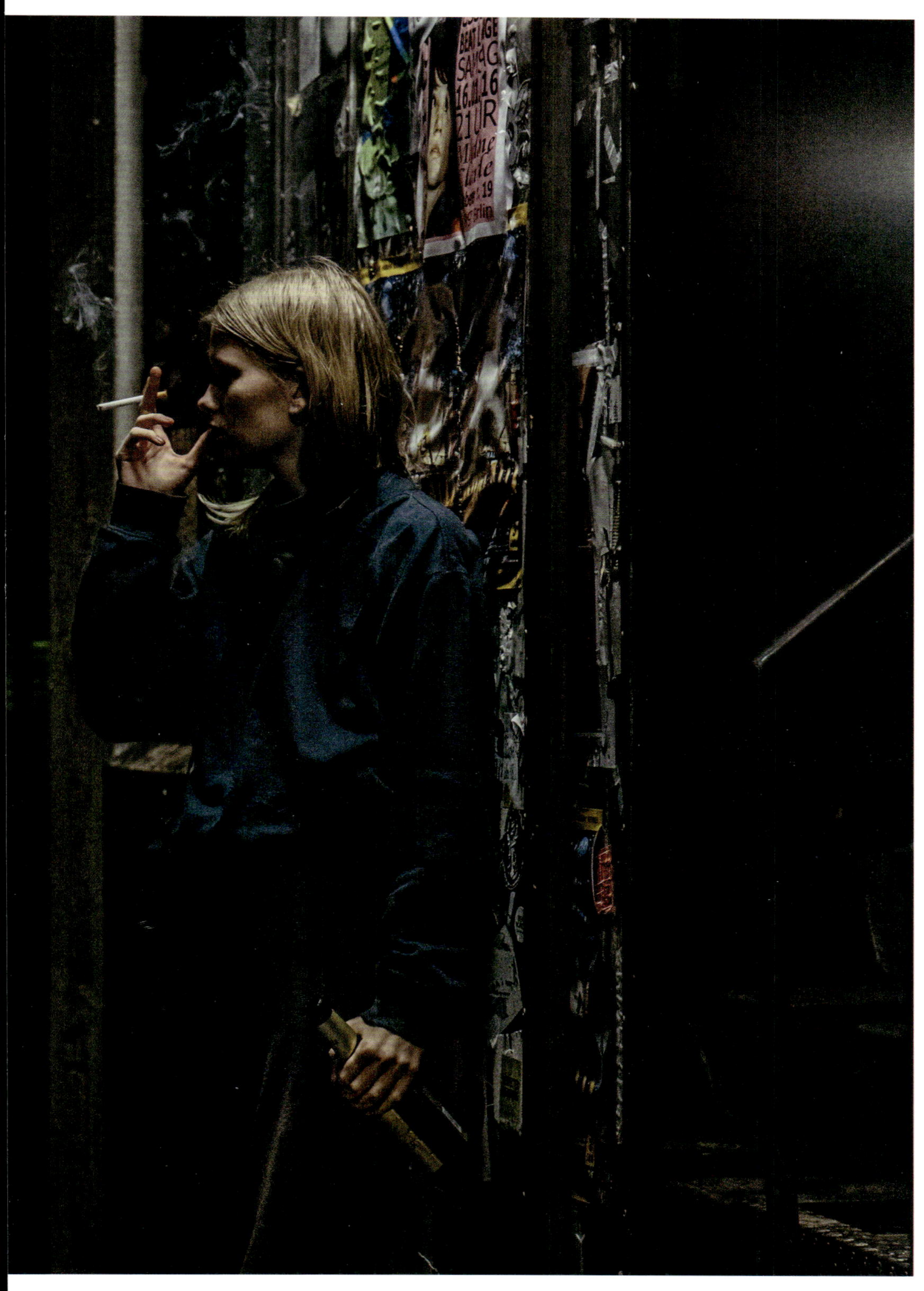

Yan Revazov

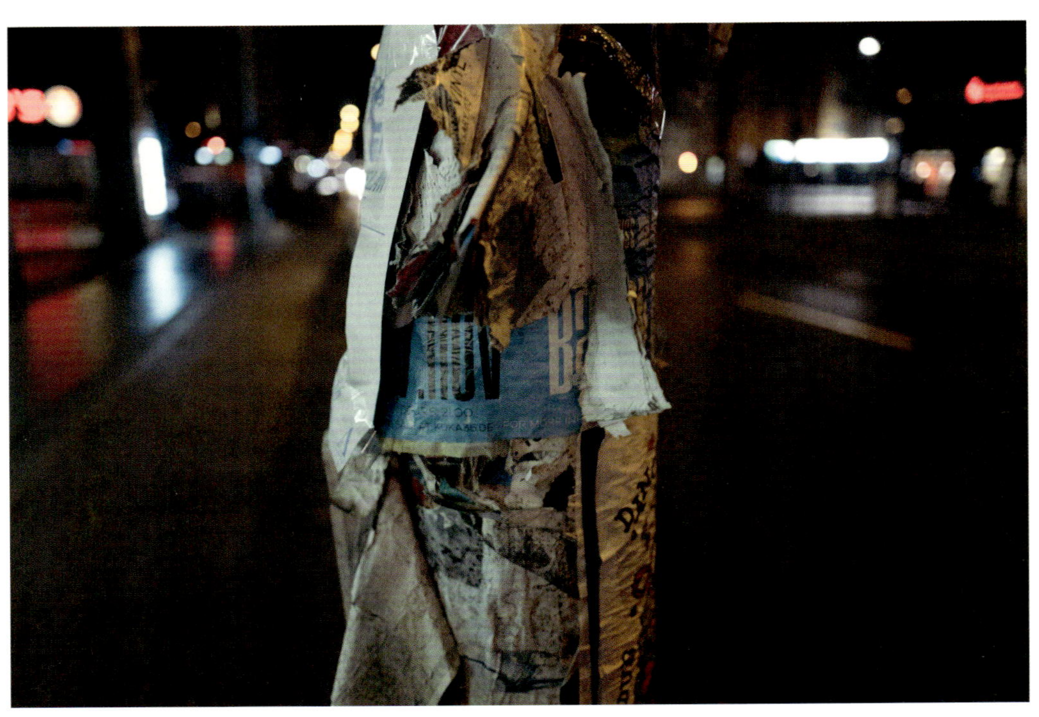

Dragica Carlin

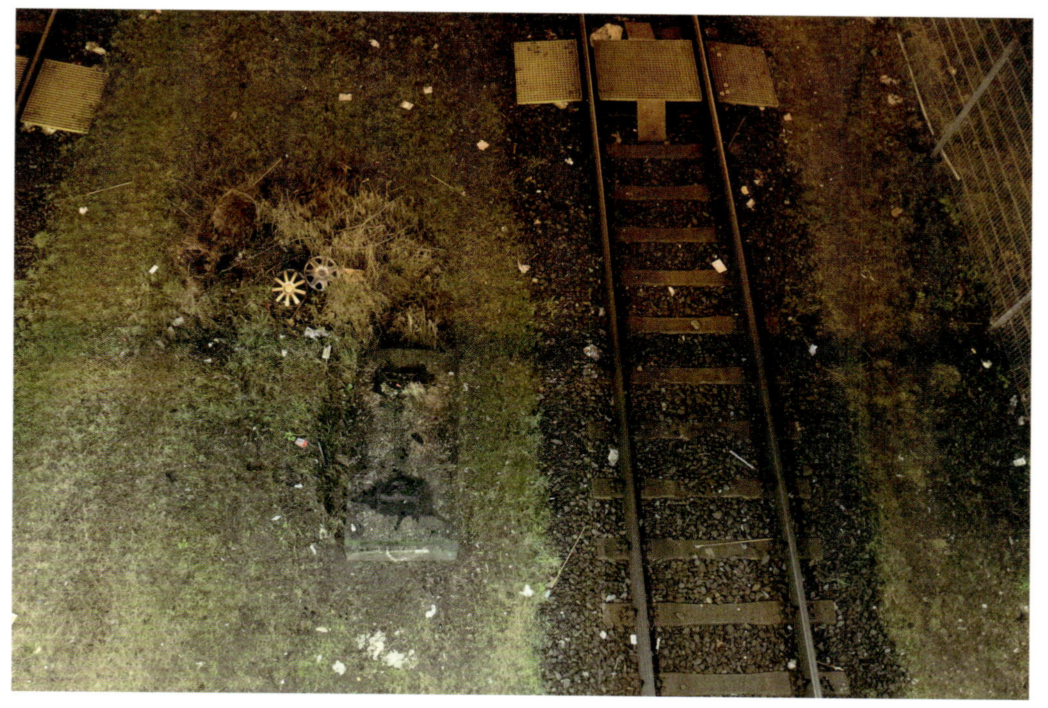

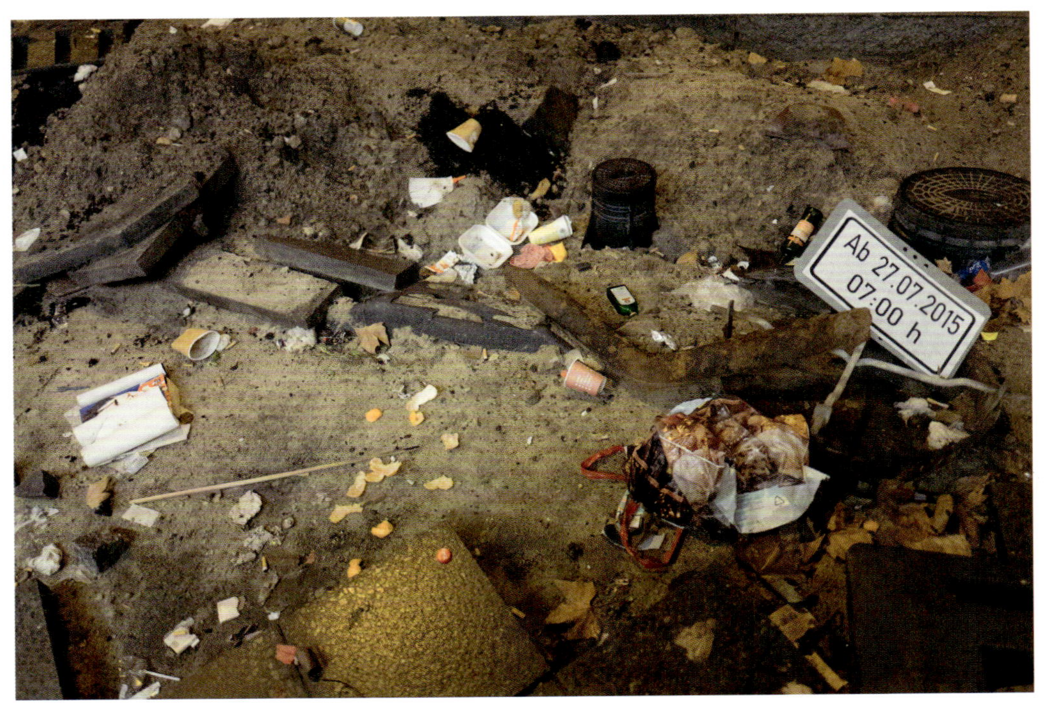

Dragica Carlin

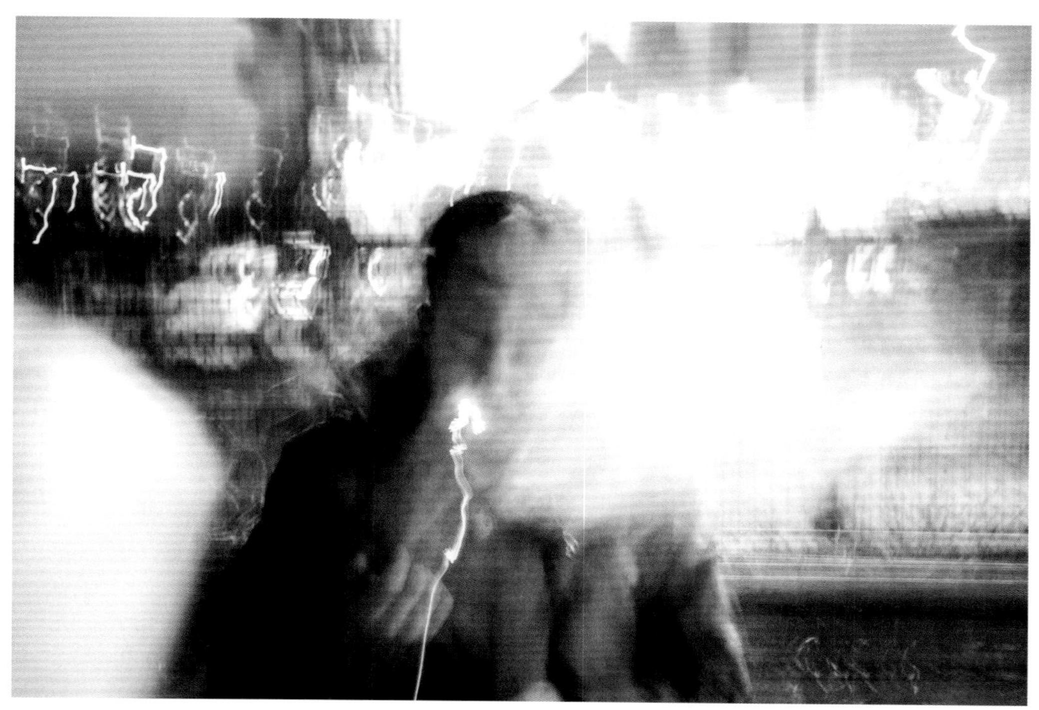

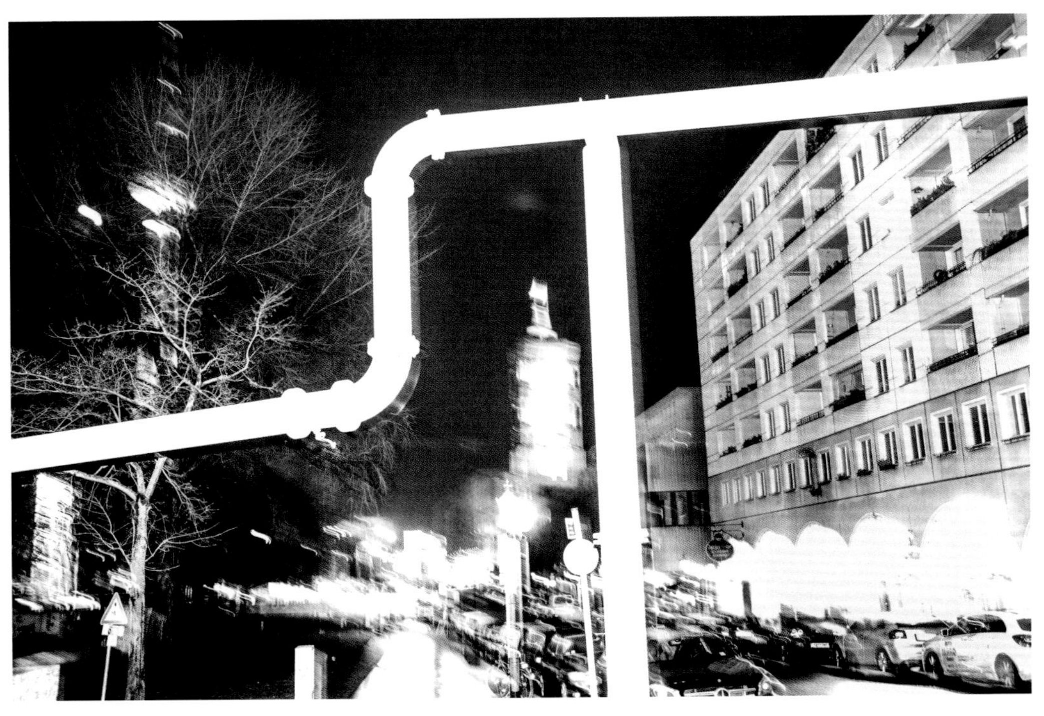

Gabriele Micalizzi

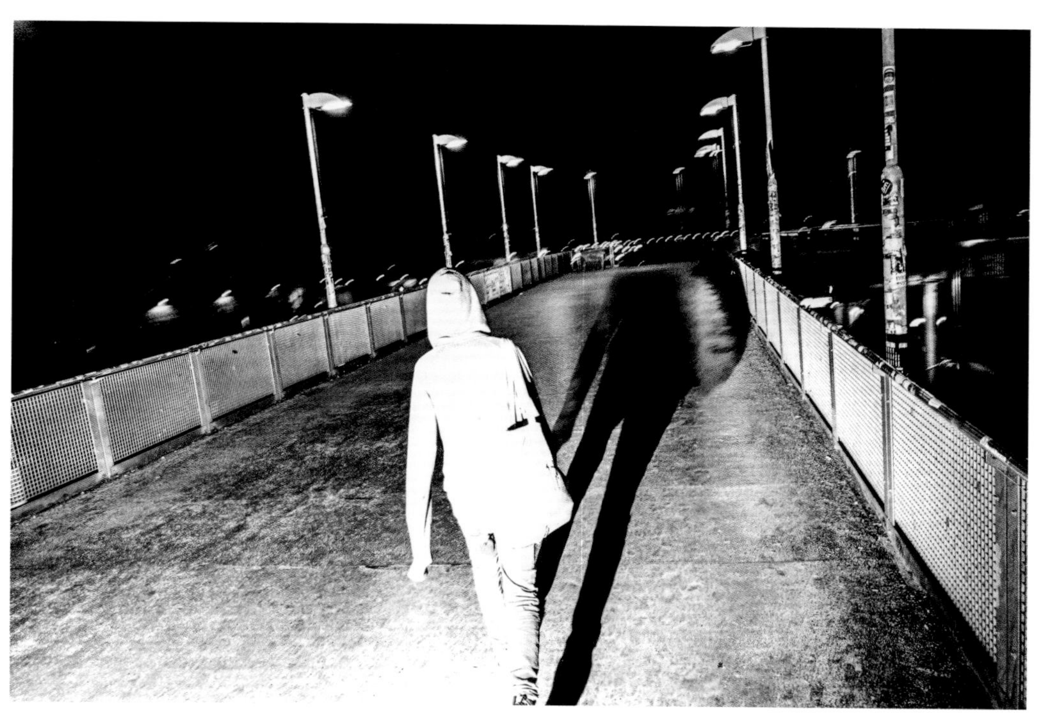

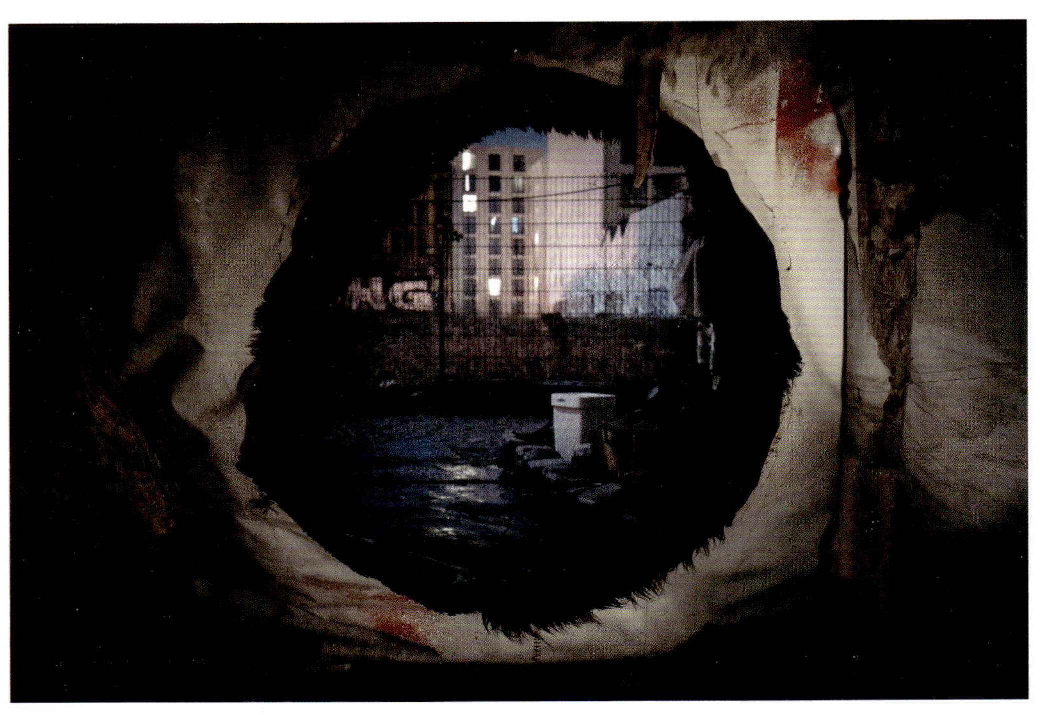

Lanka Perren

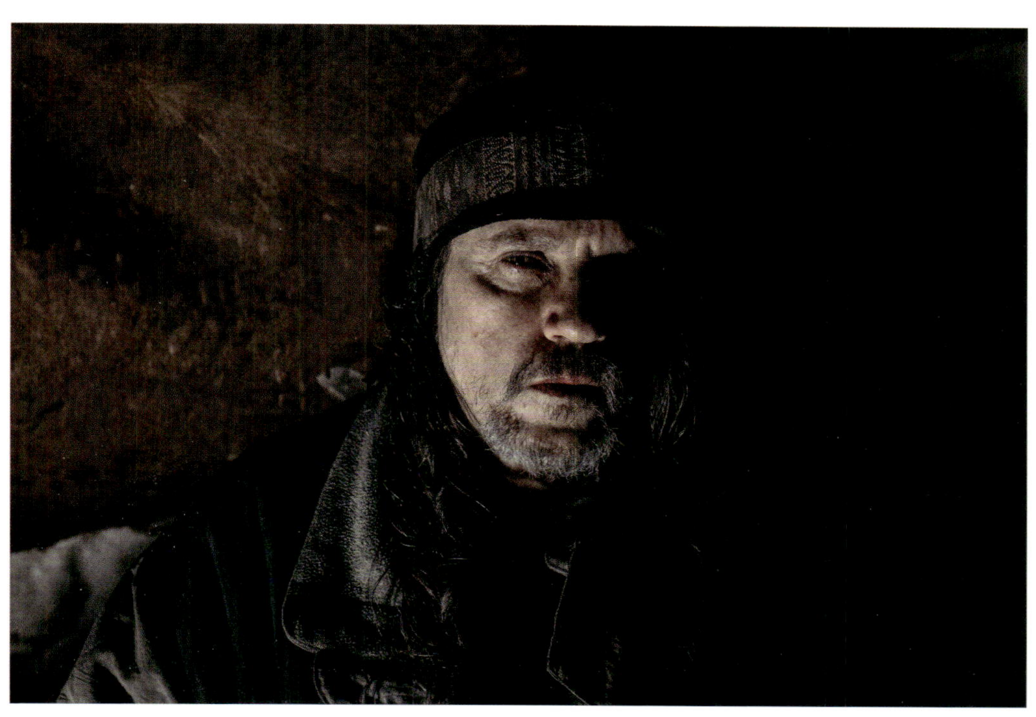

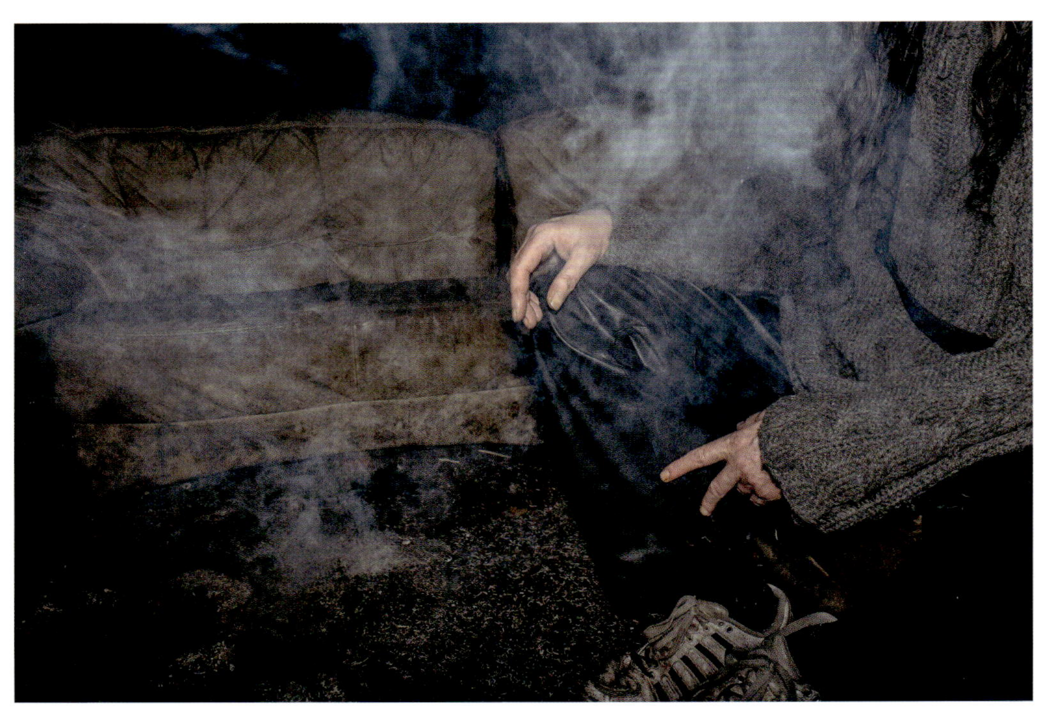

Lanka Perren

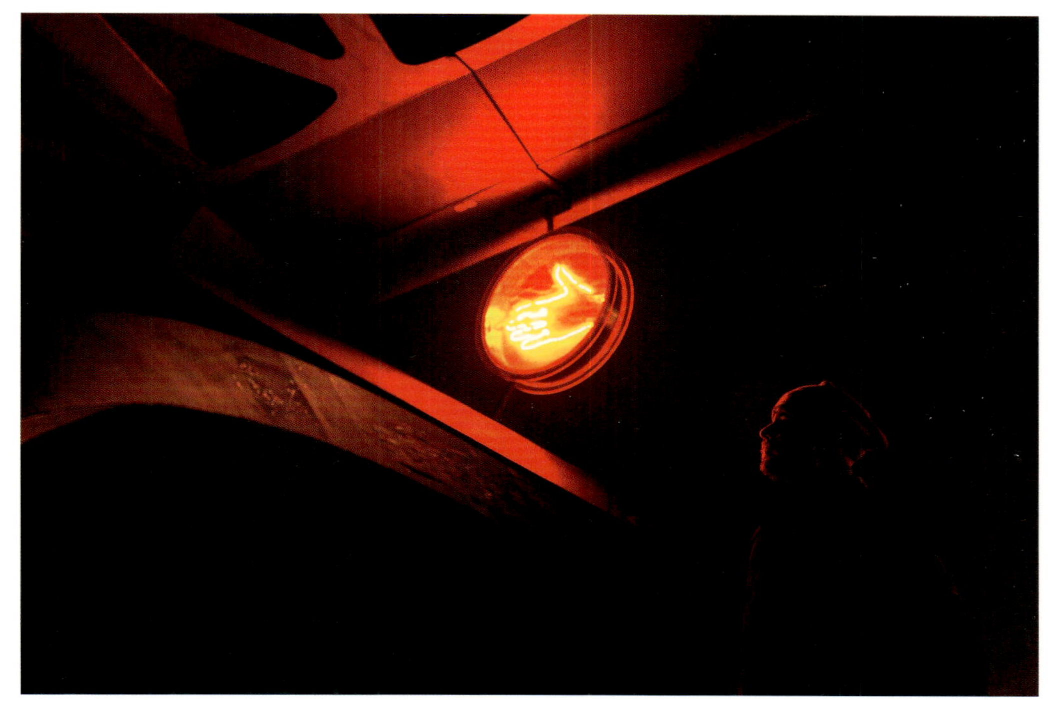

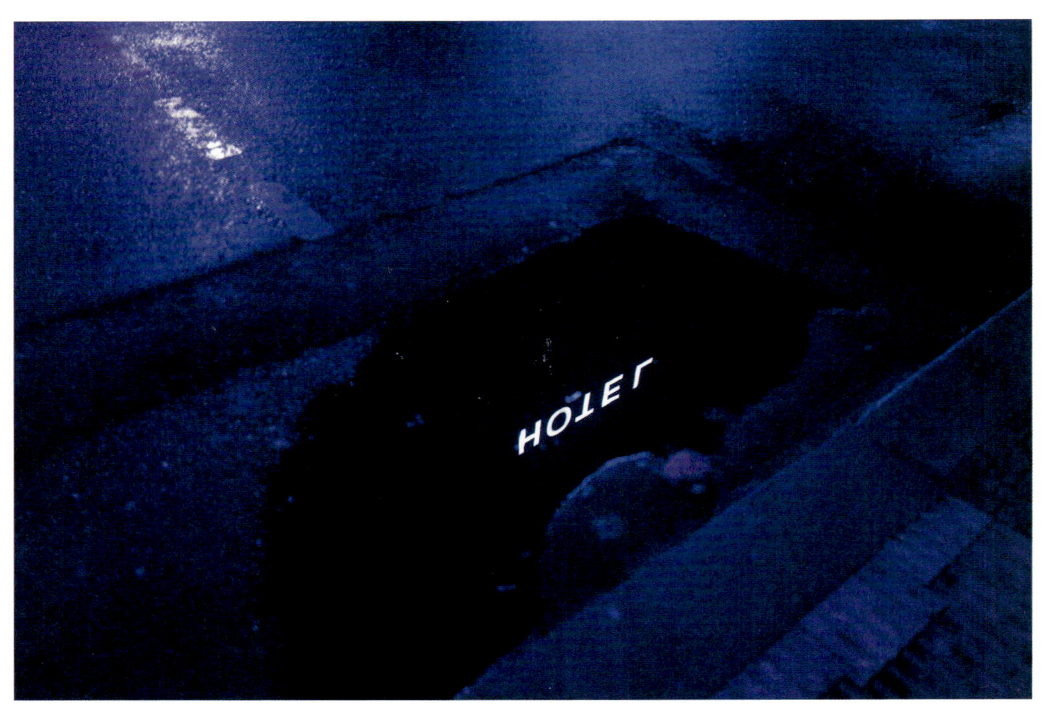

Laura Zalenga

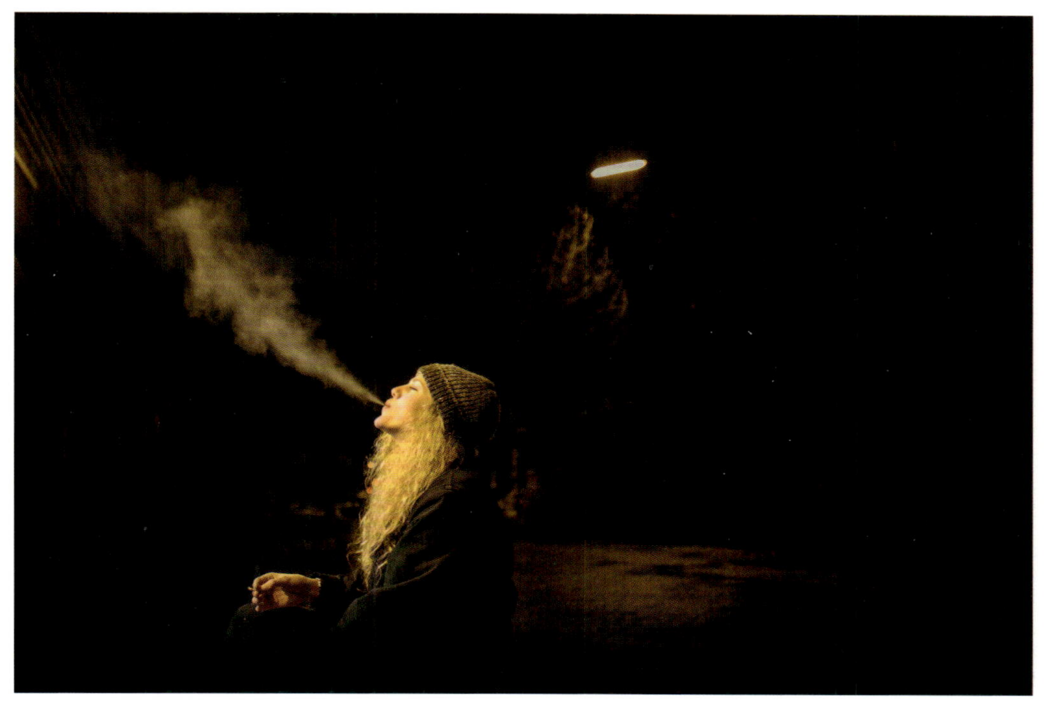

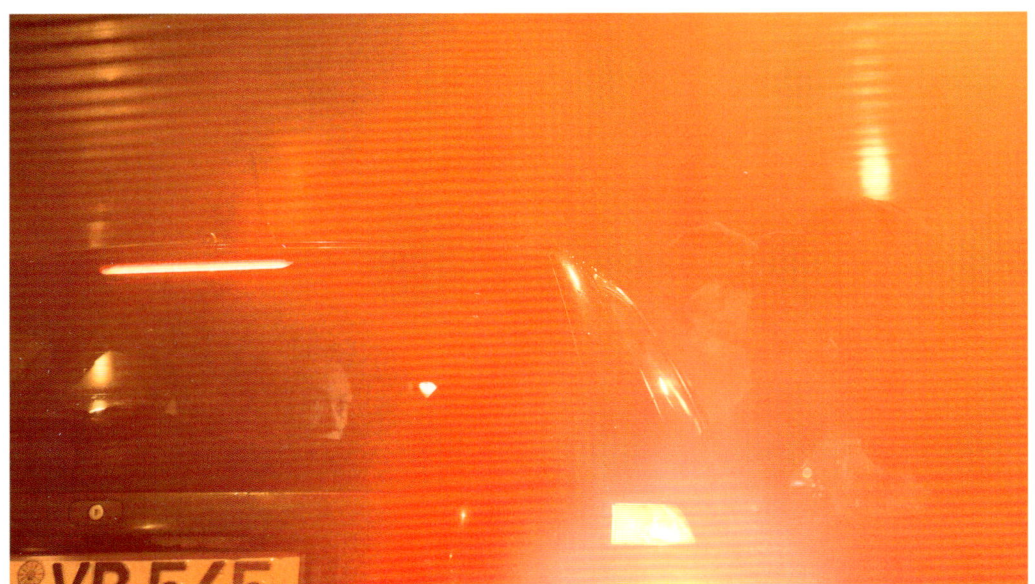

Sebastian Siebel

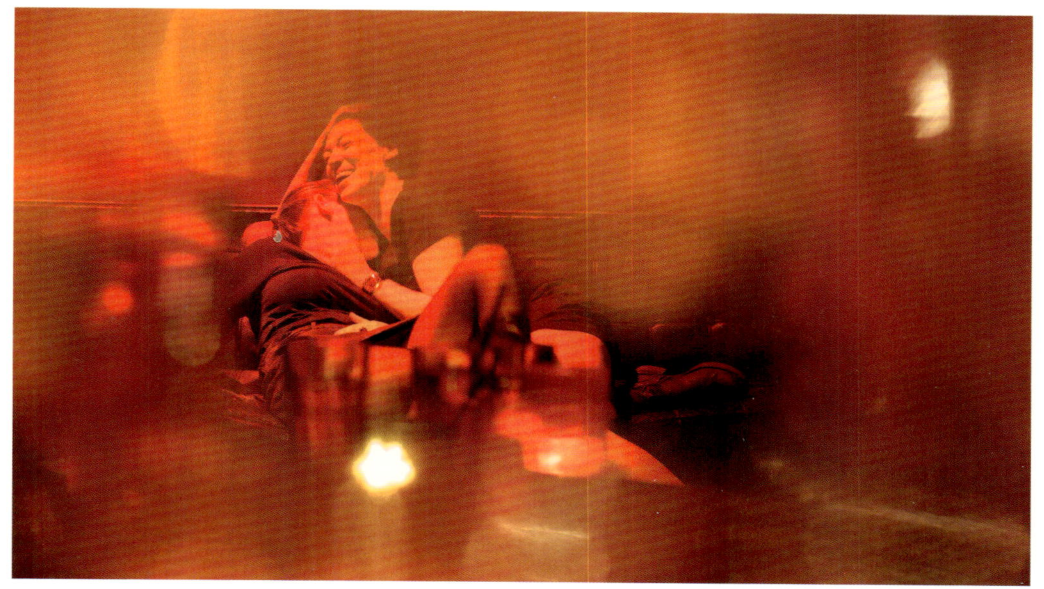

Sebastian Siebel

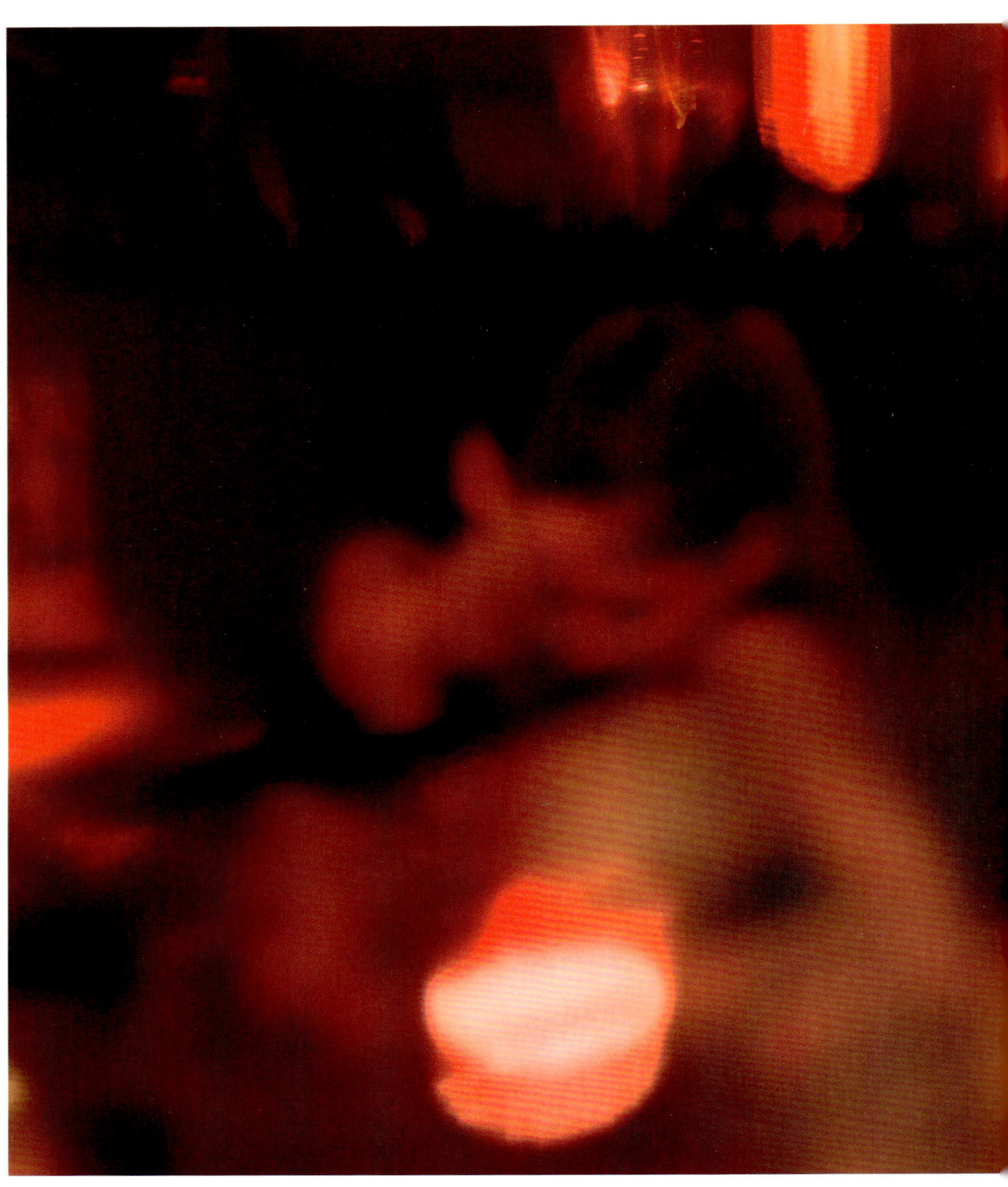

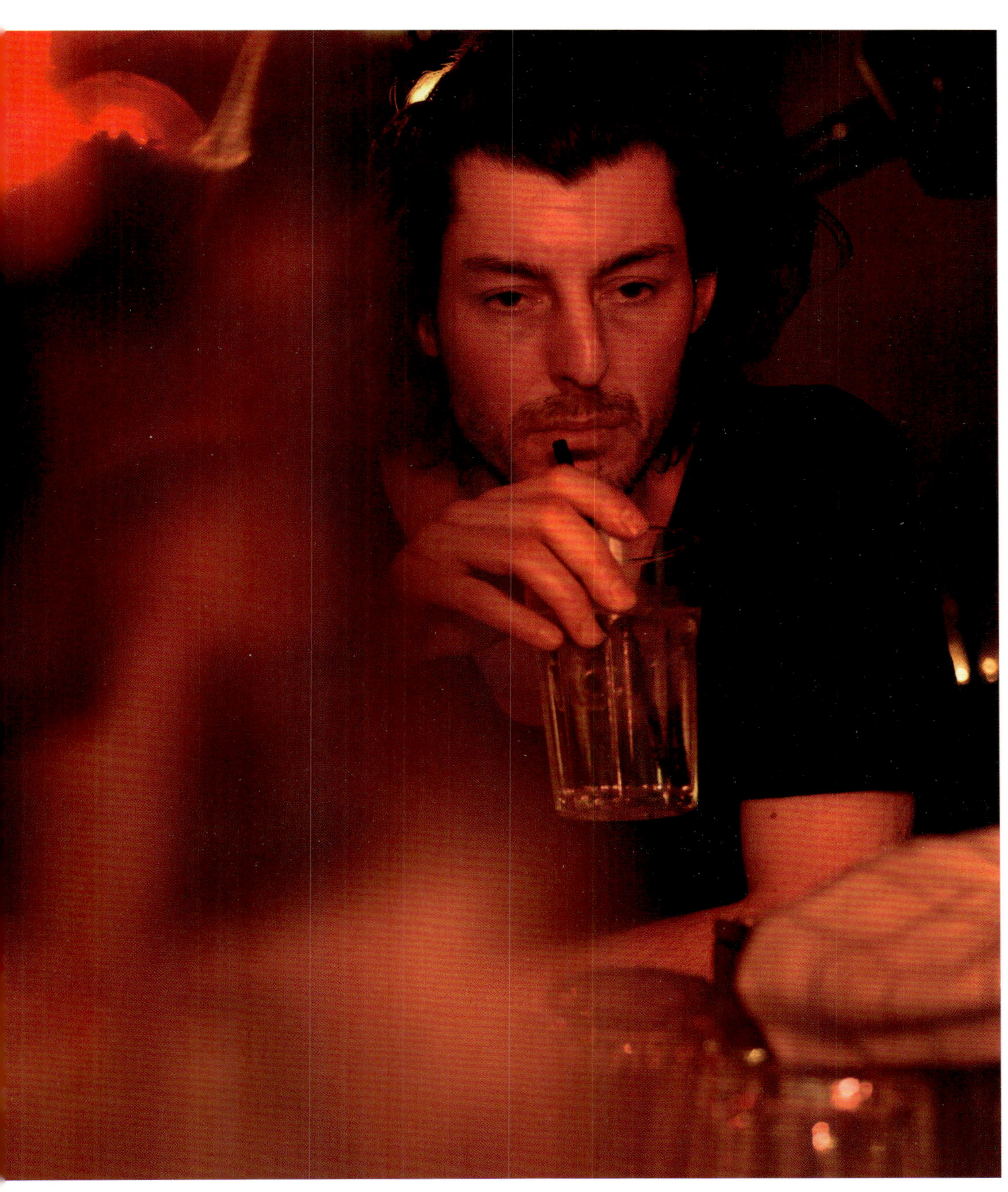

Sebastian Siebel

THE BODY

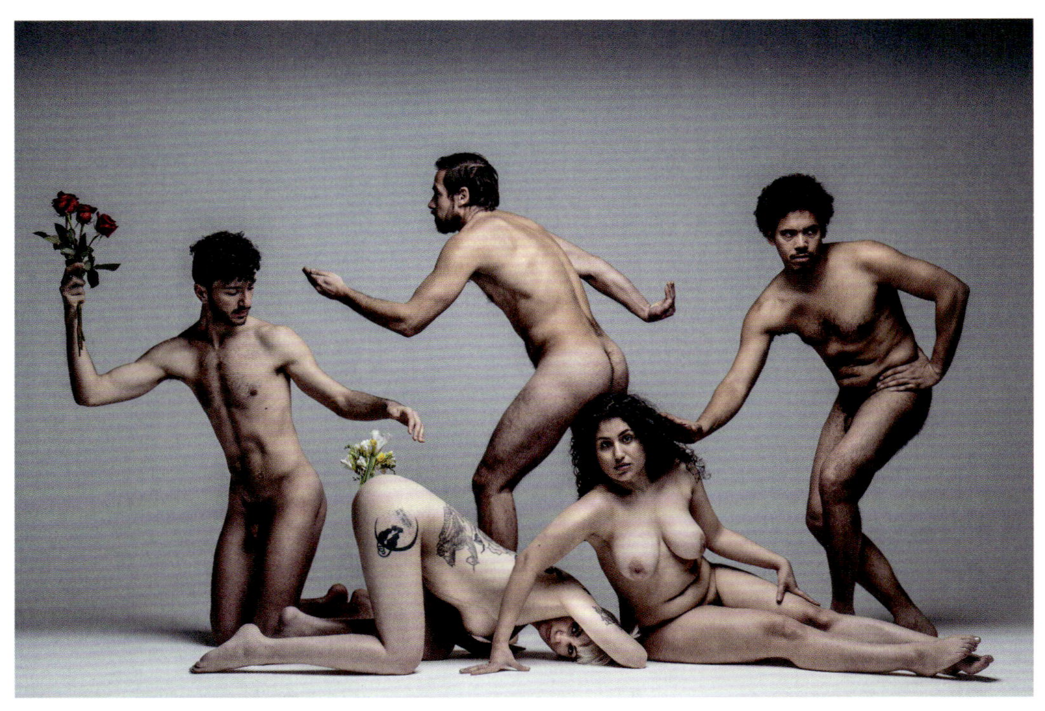

Marta Lallana García

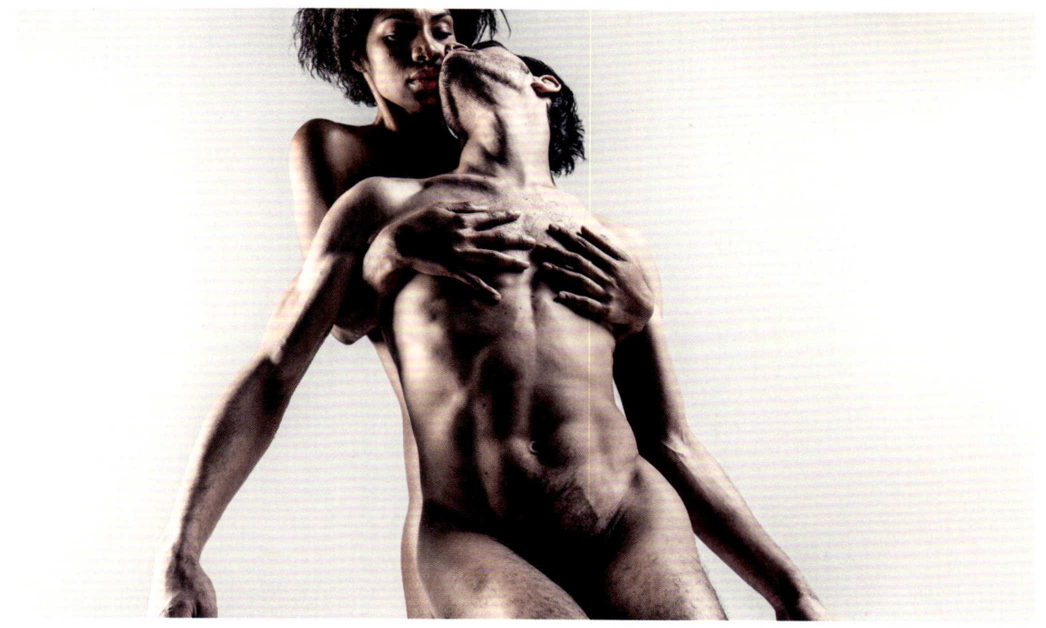

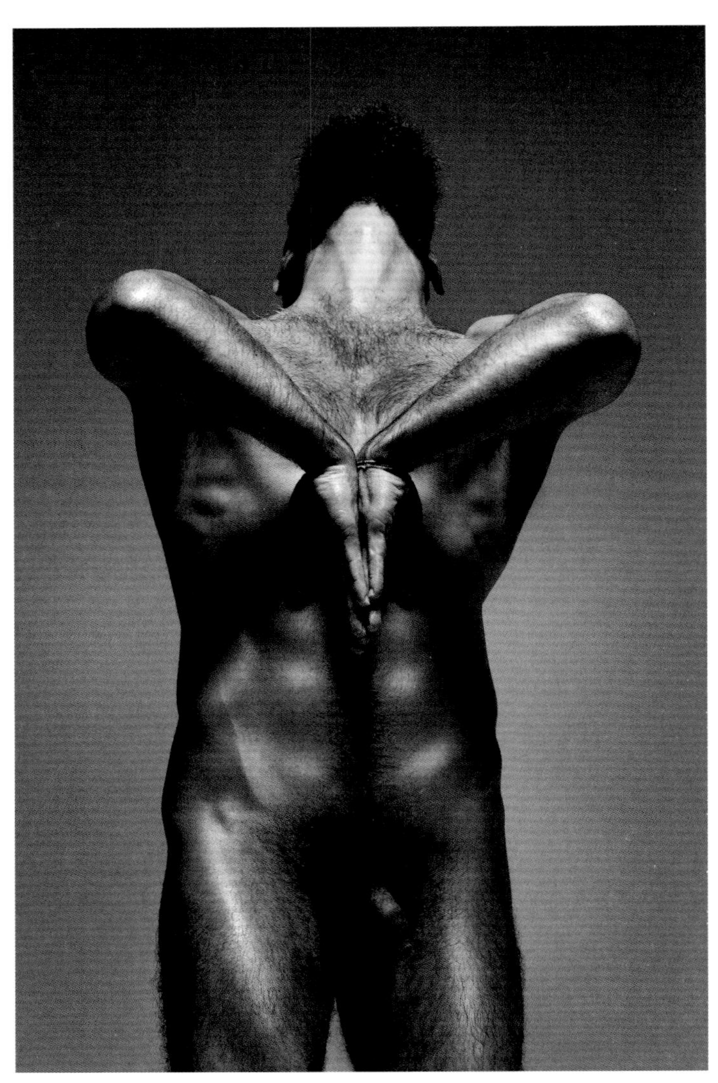

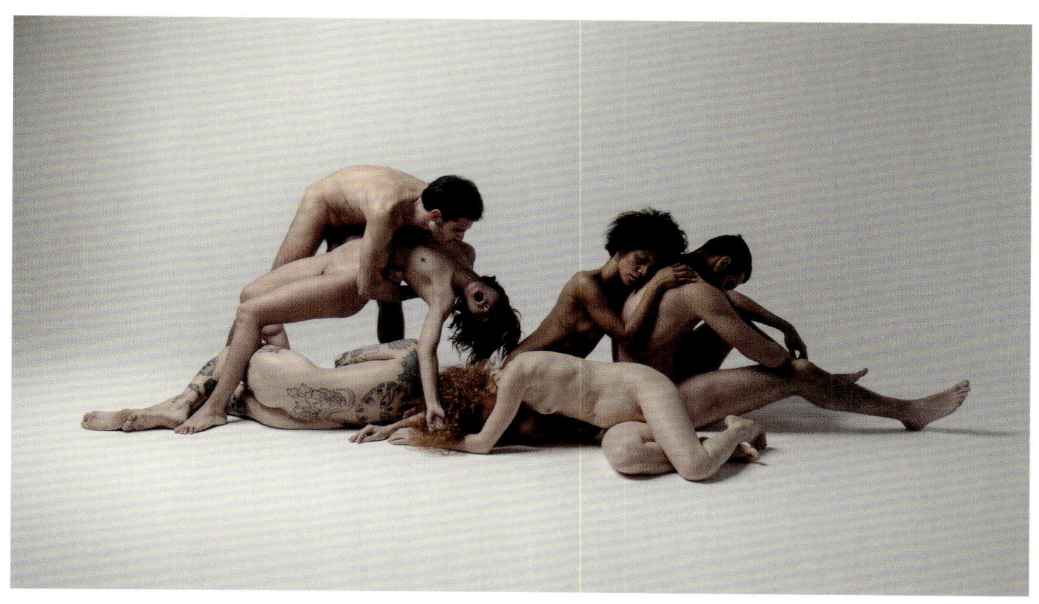

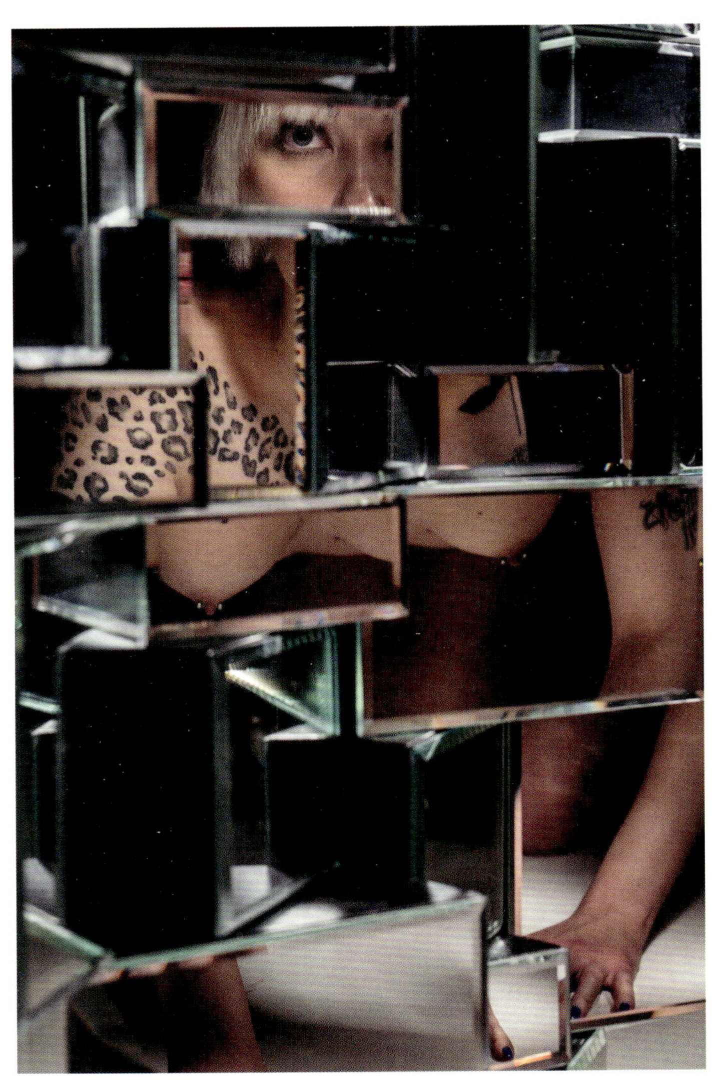

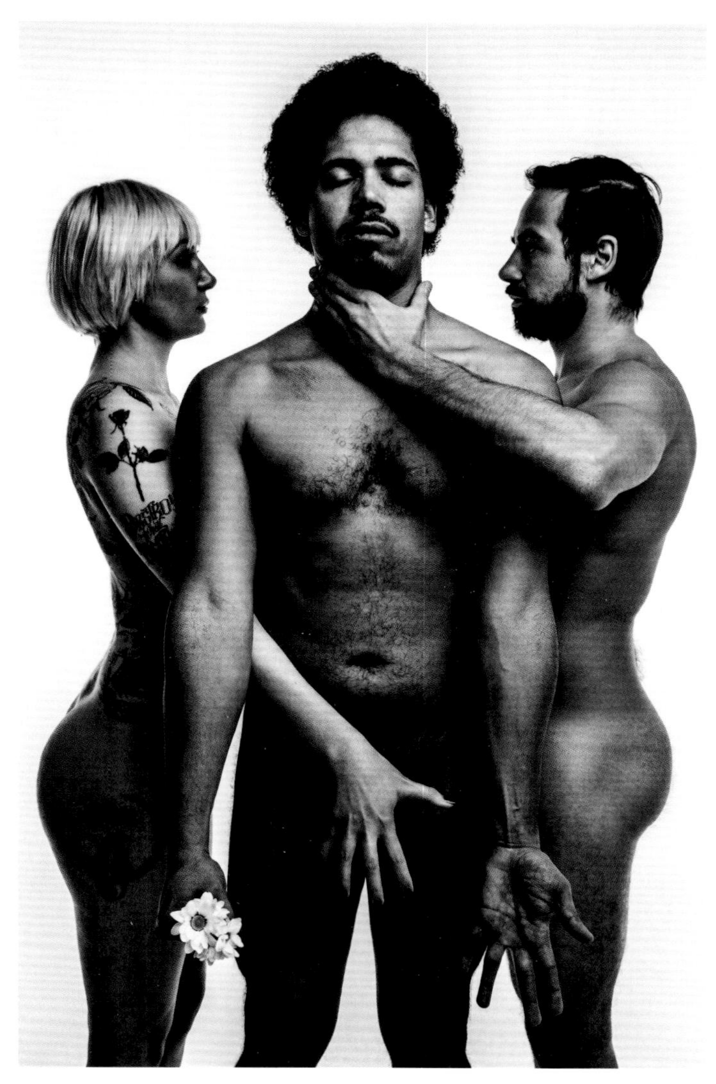

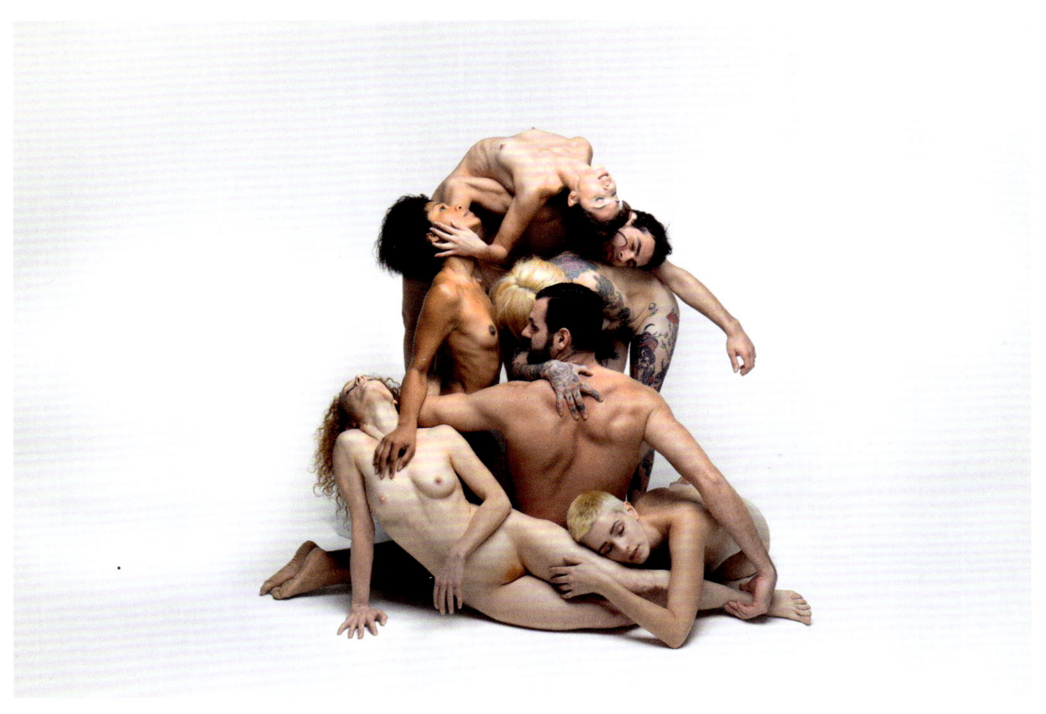

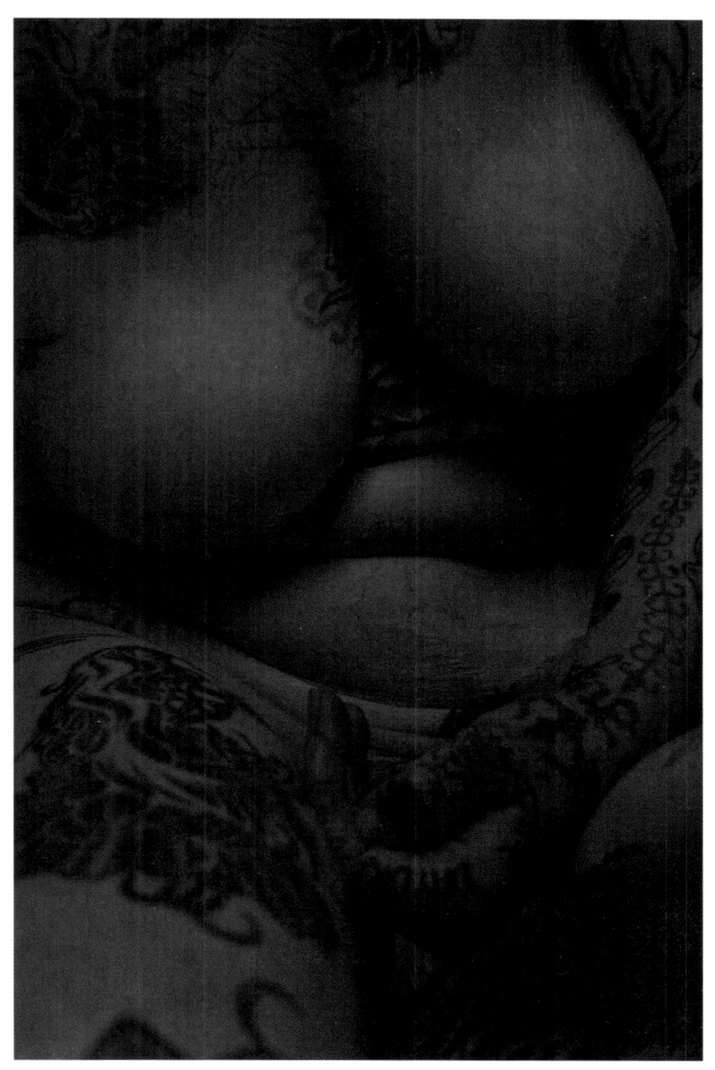

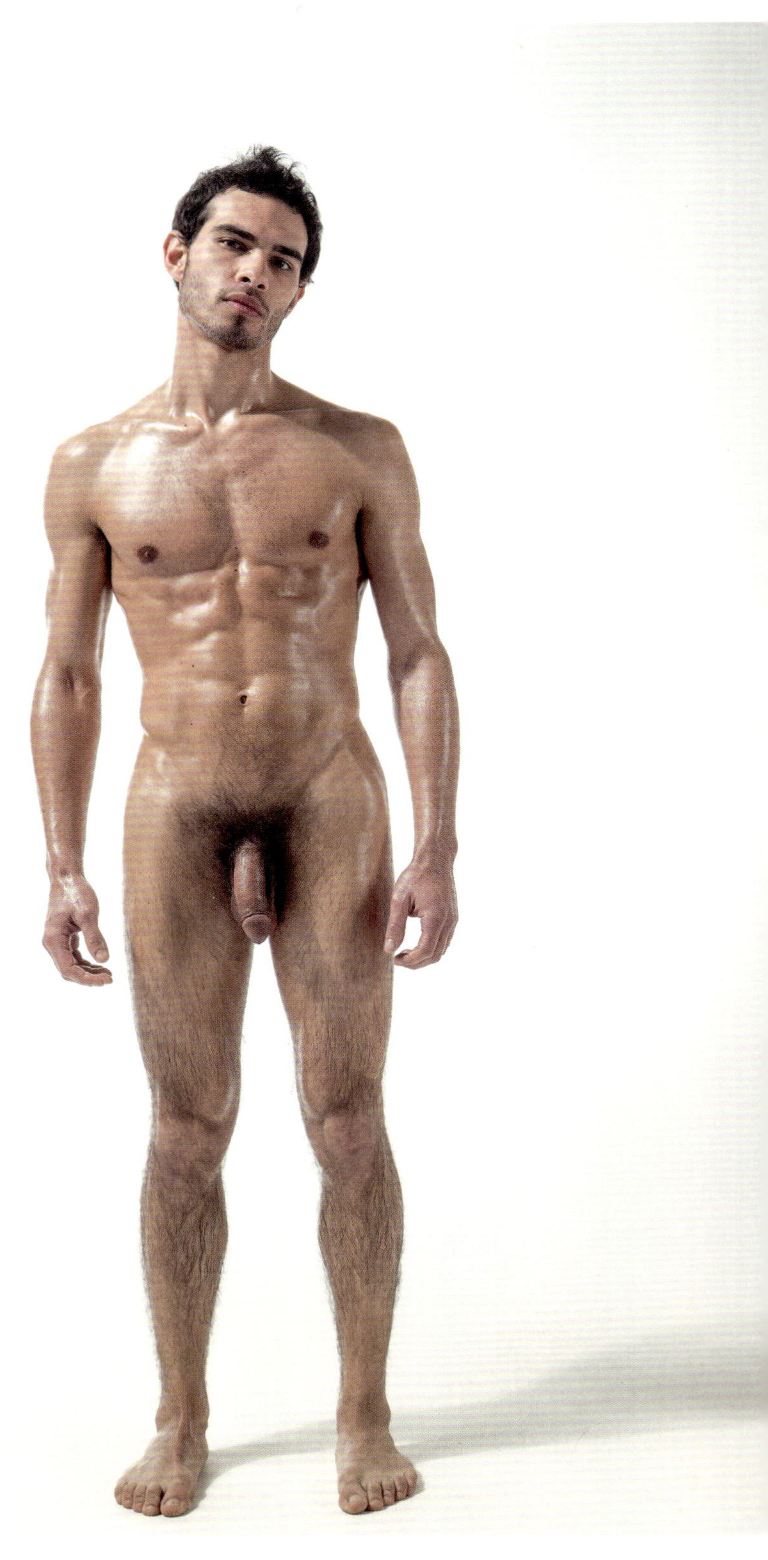

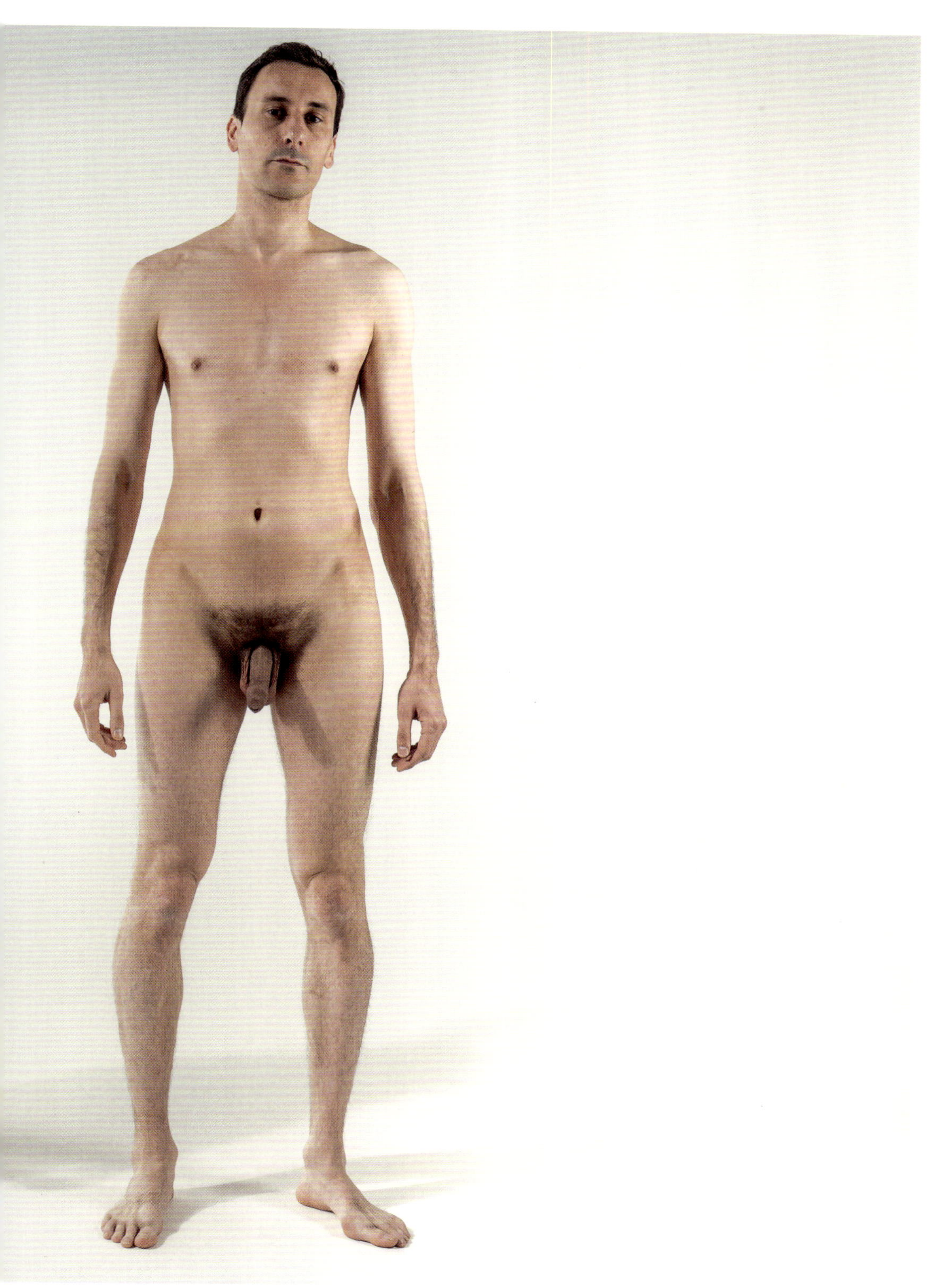

Lanka Perren

CELEBRITY PORTRAIT

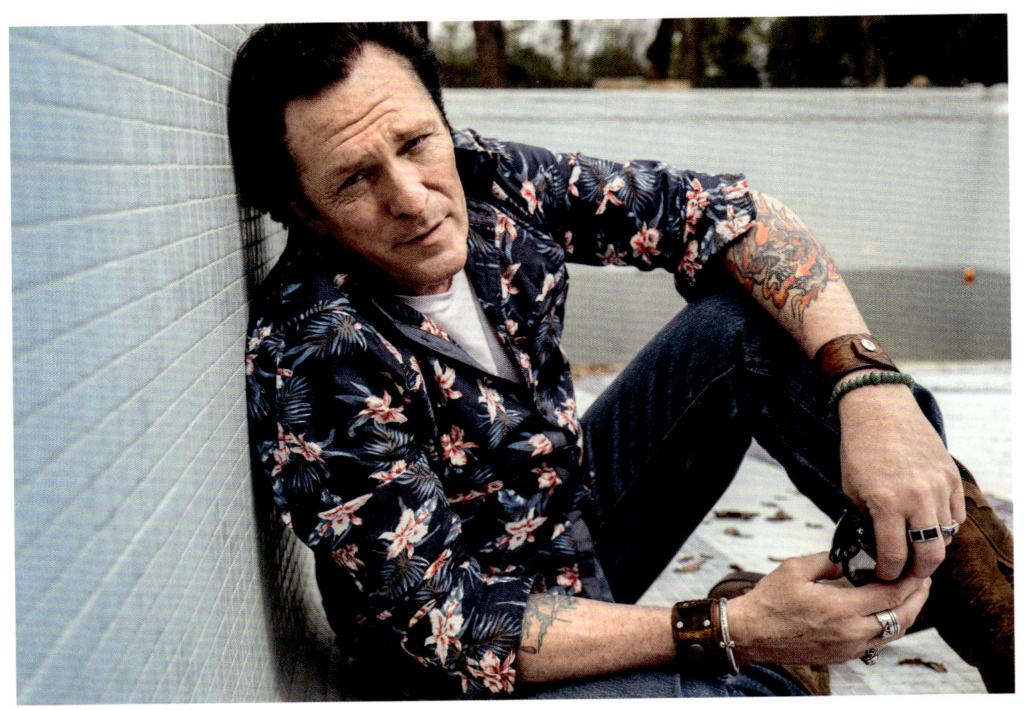

Rupert Frere

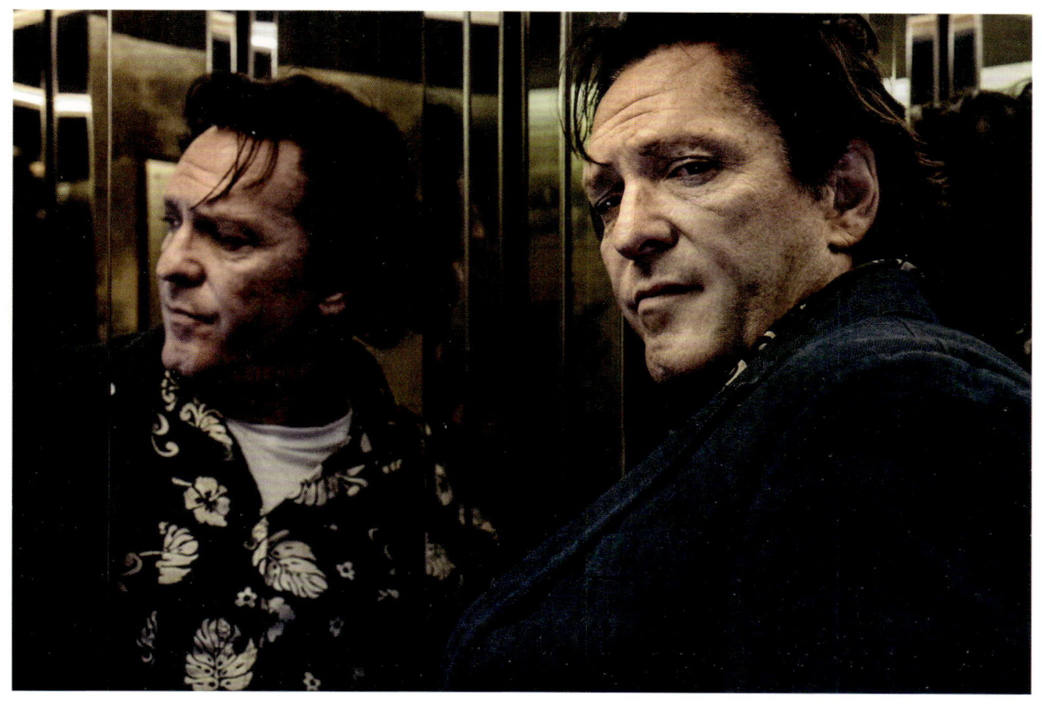

Mary Stuart

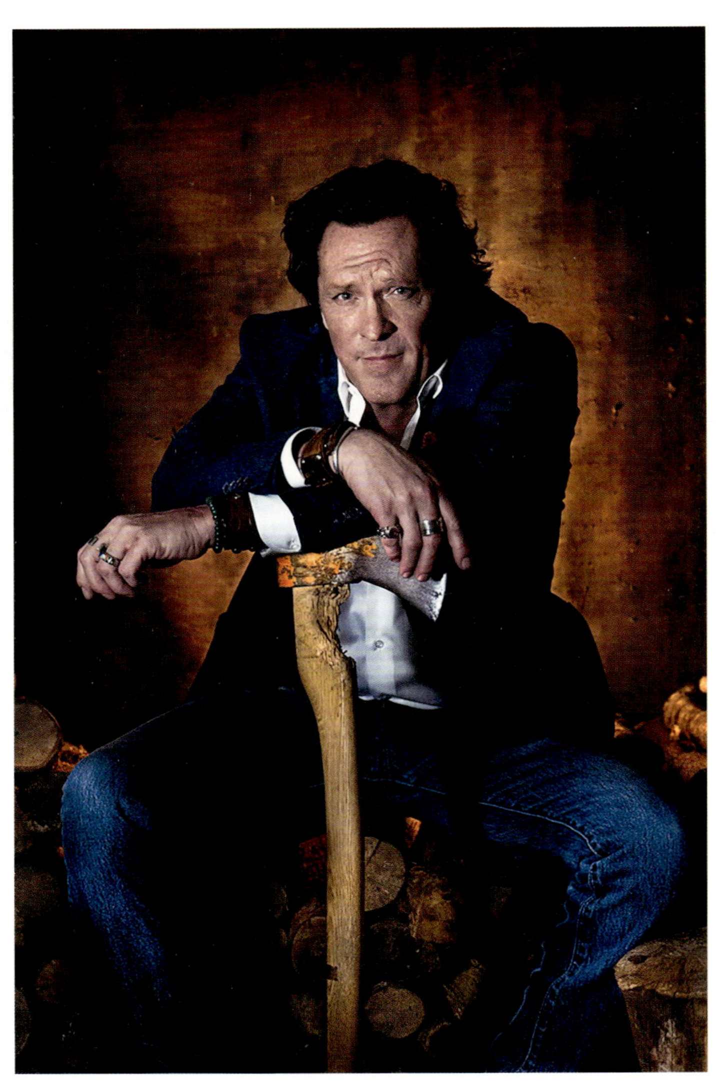

Yan Revazov

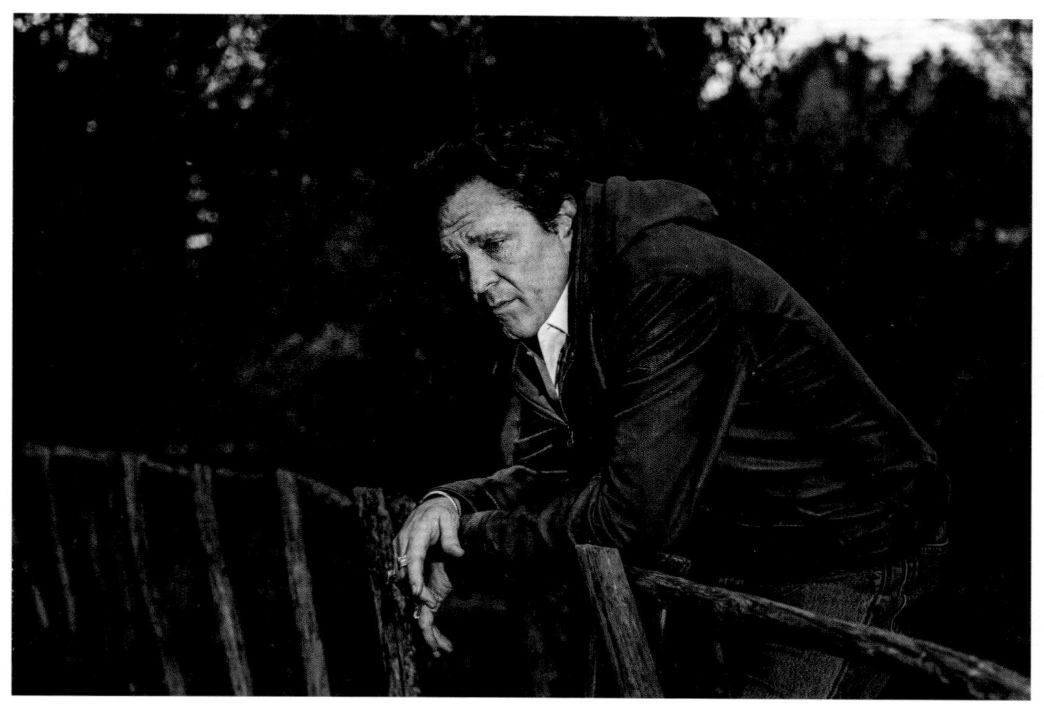

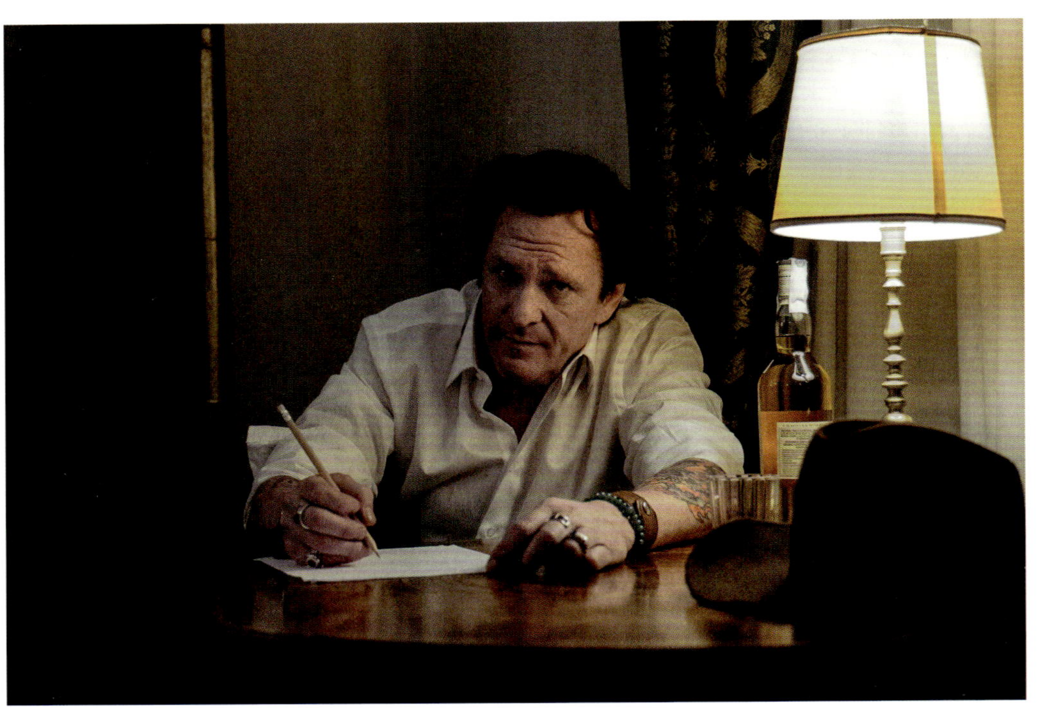

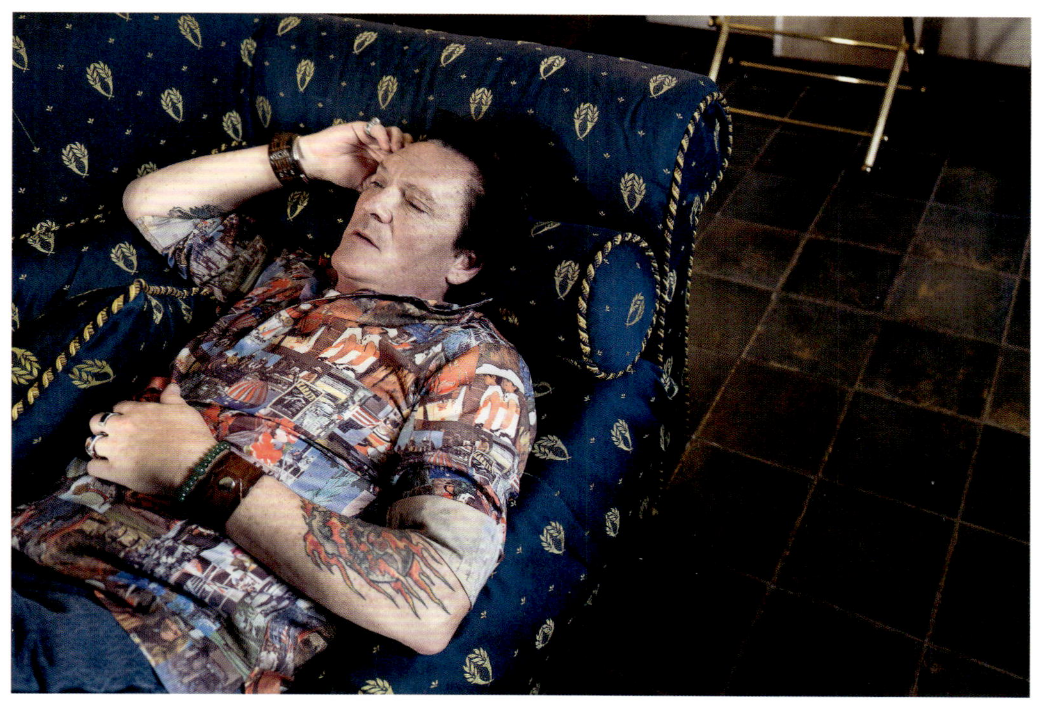

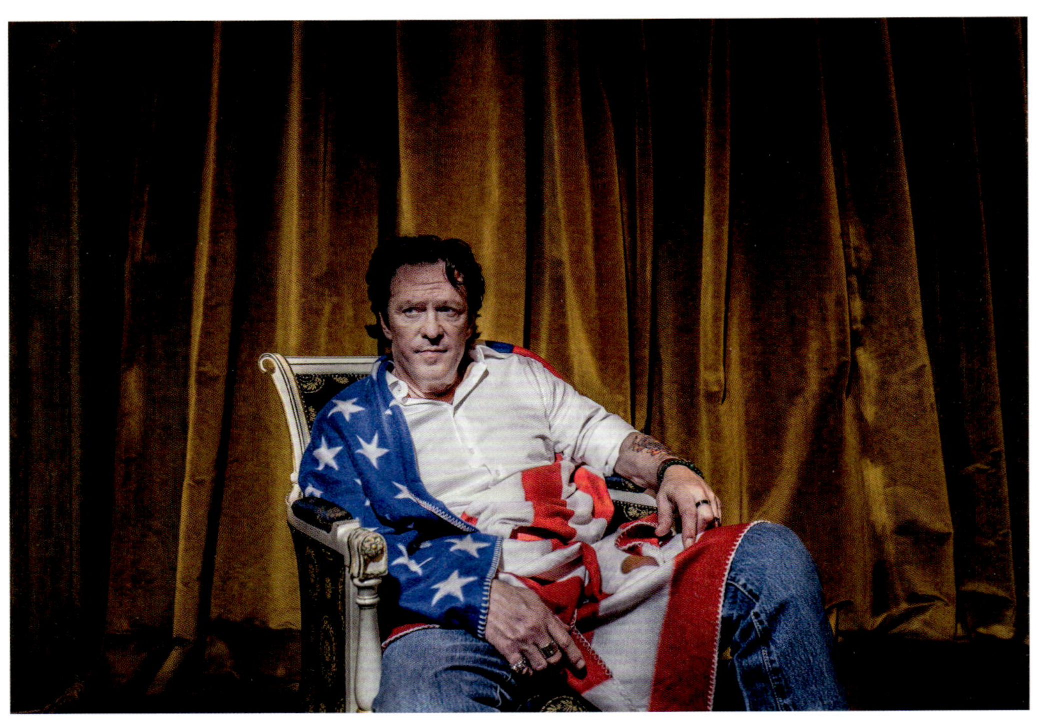

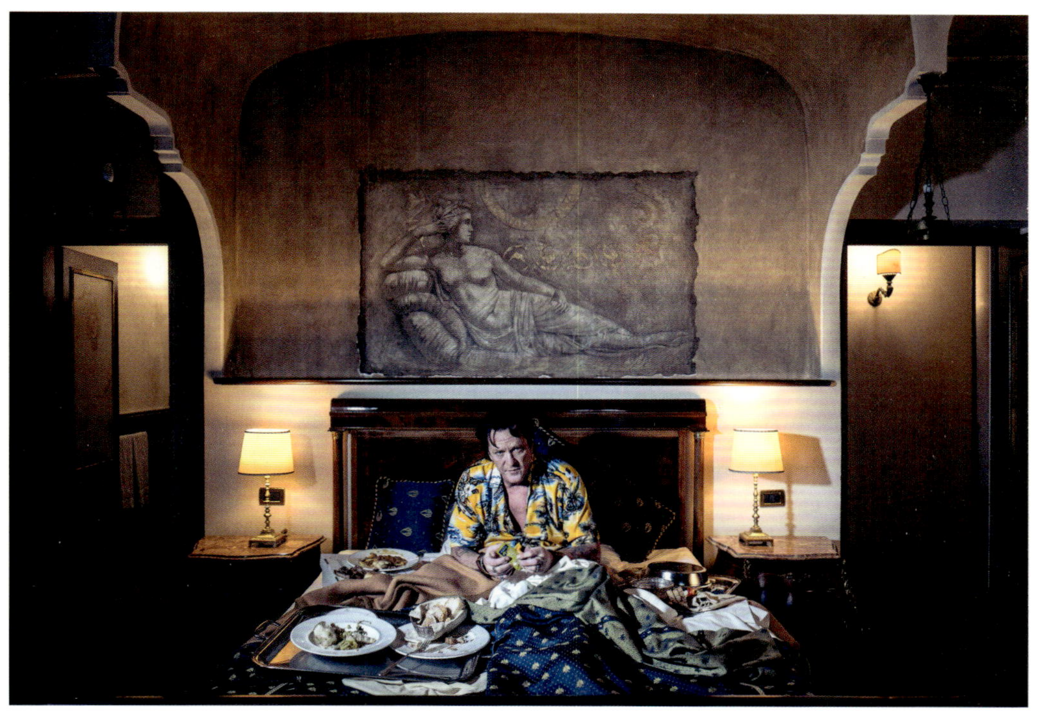

LONDON BACKSTAGE

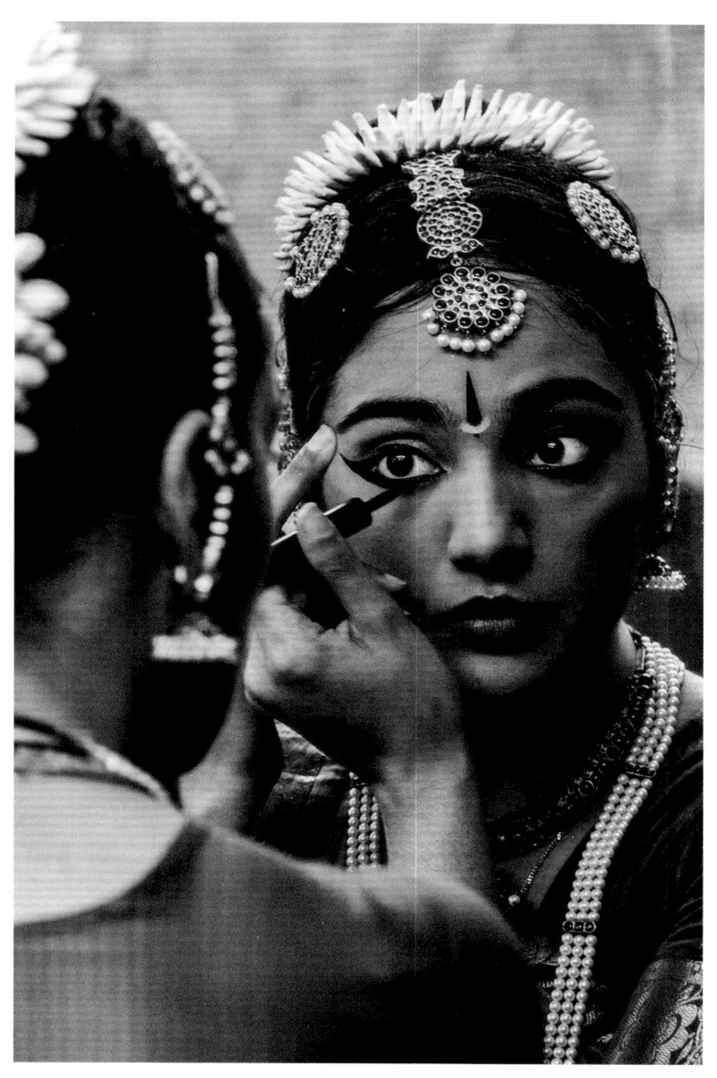

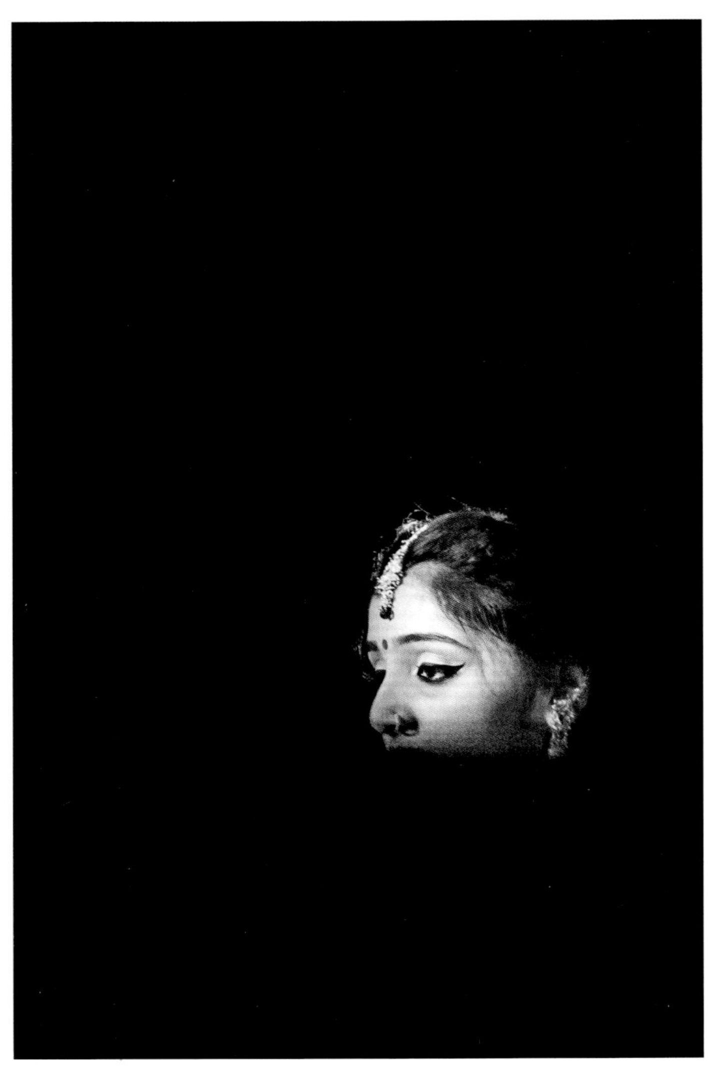

Neal Gruer

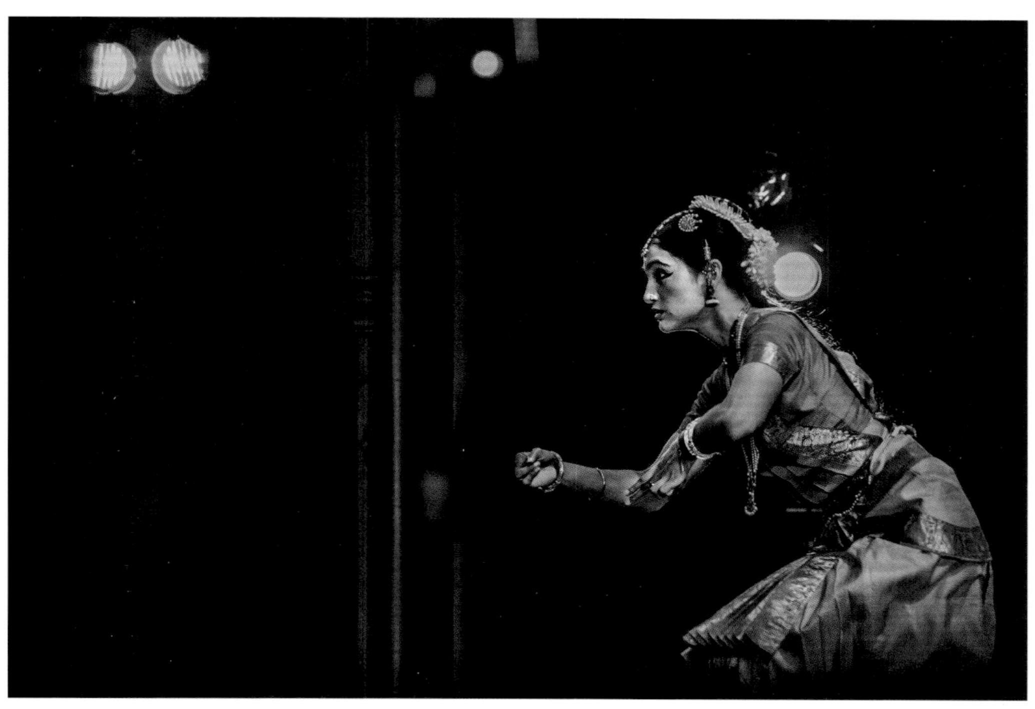

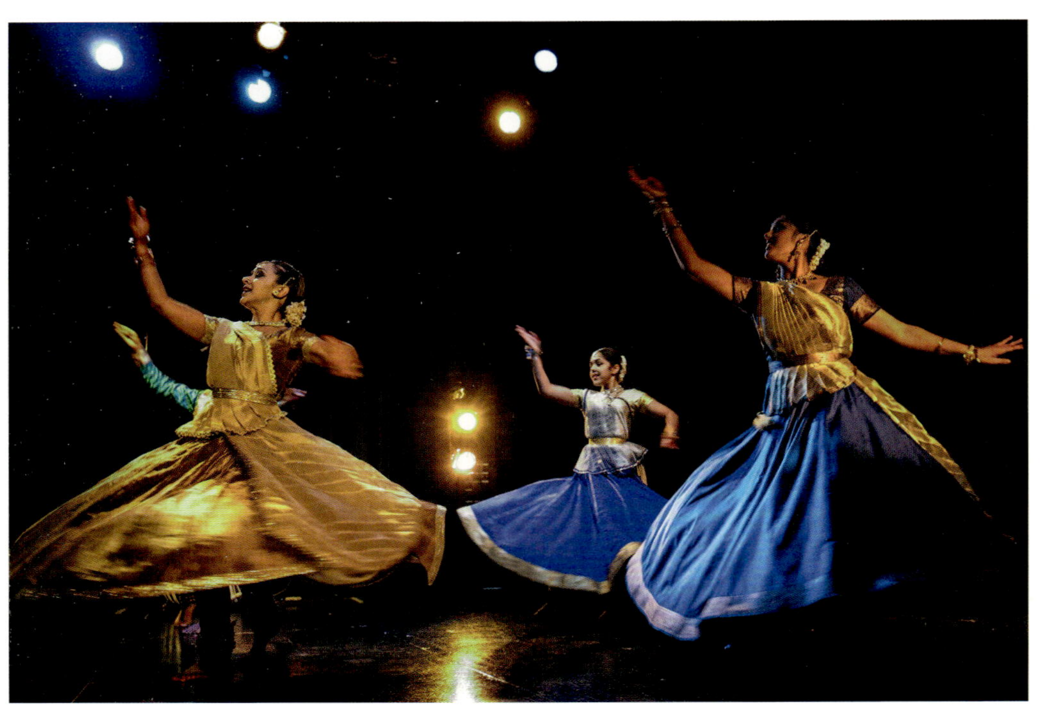

Mary Stuart

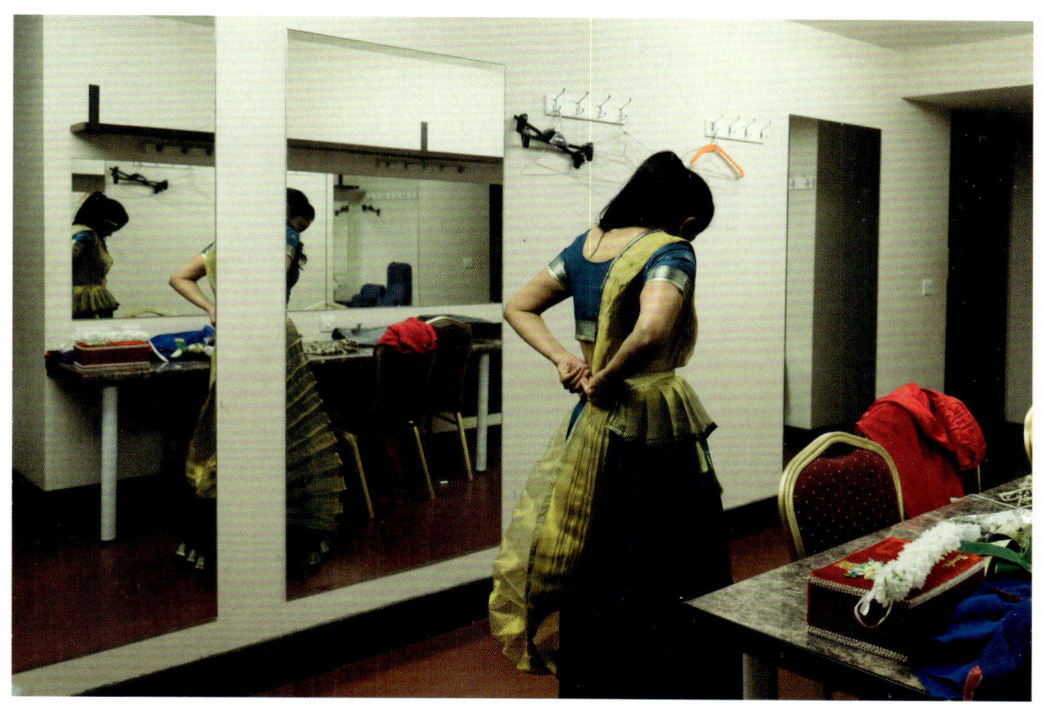

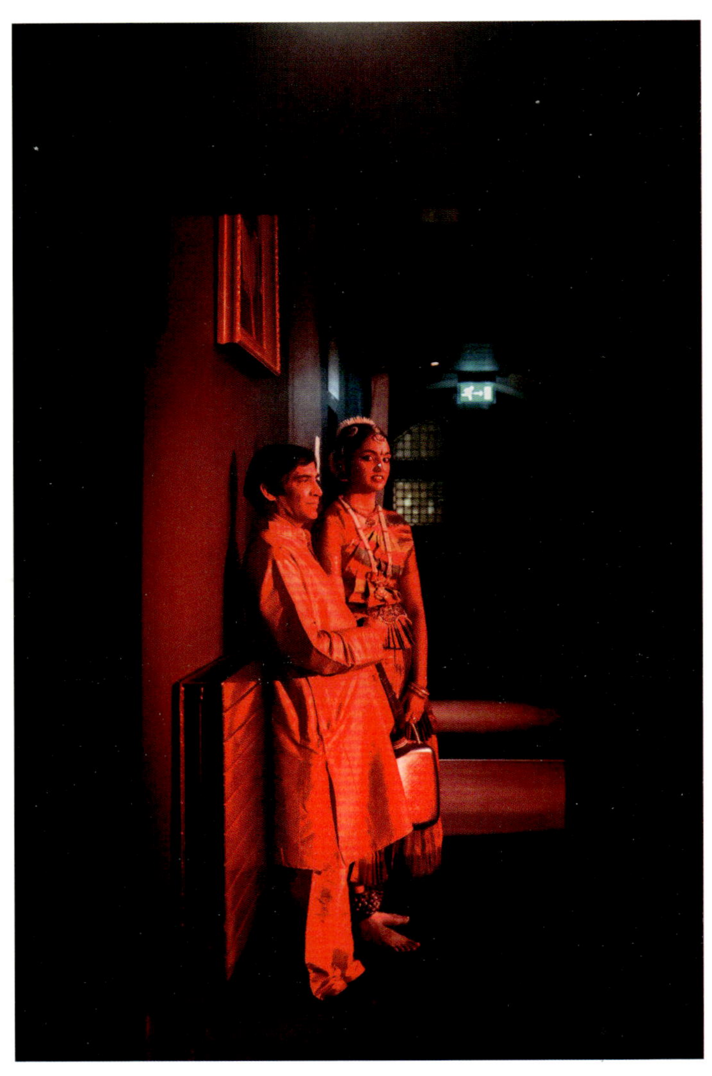

Mary Stuart

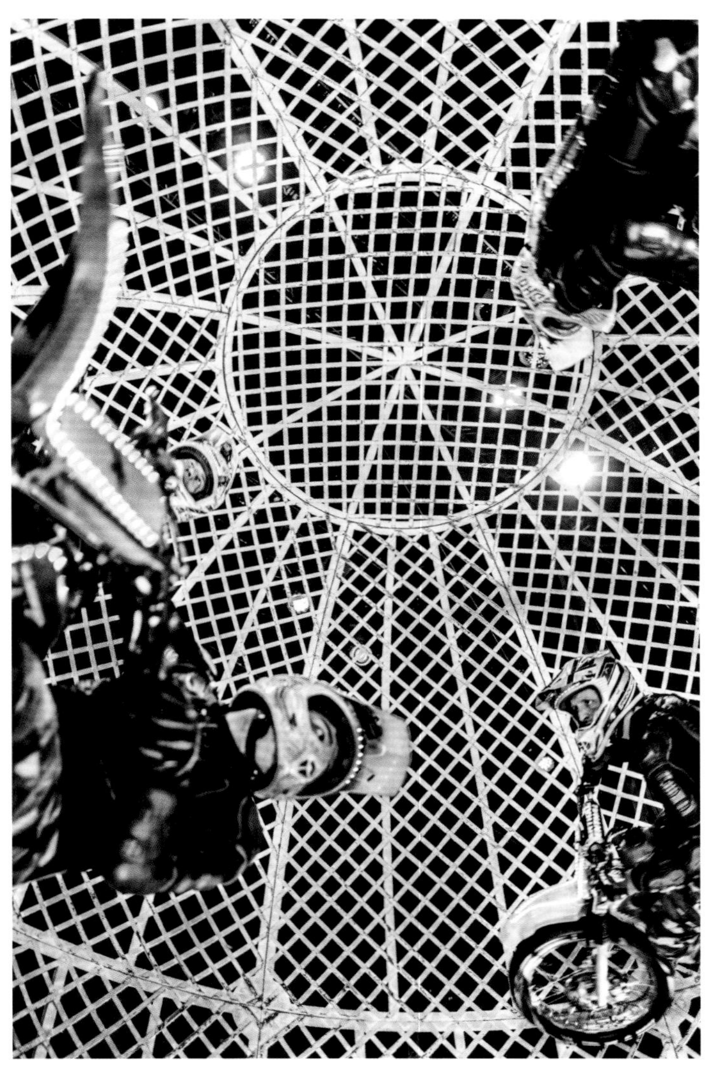

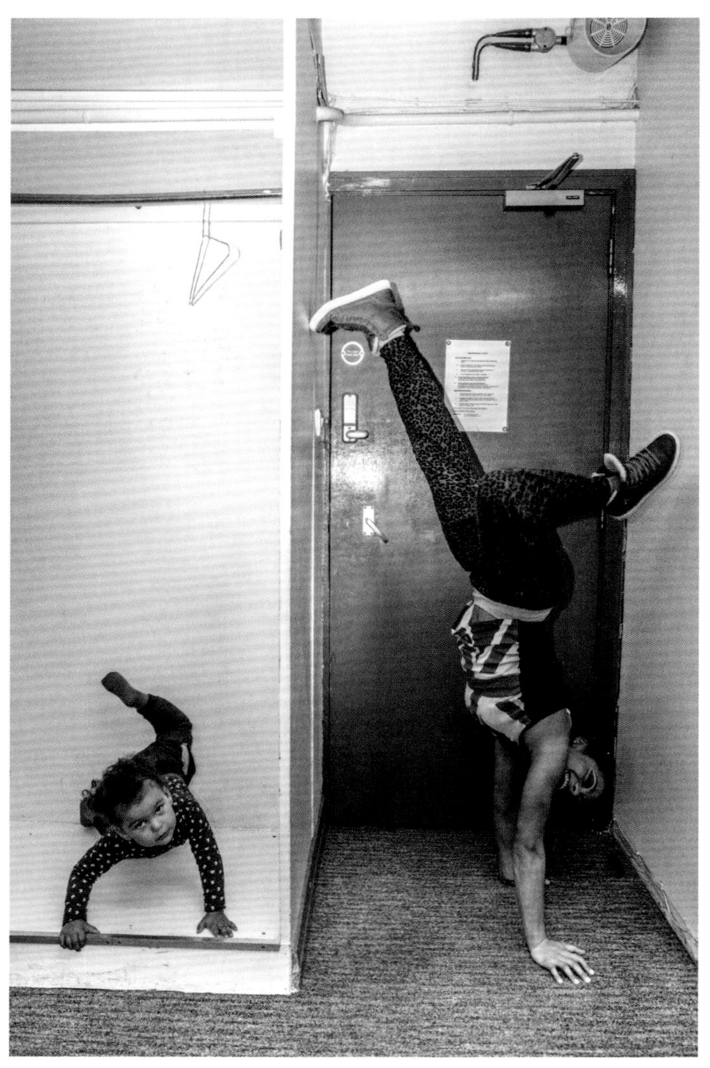

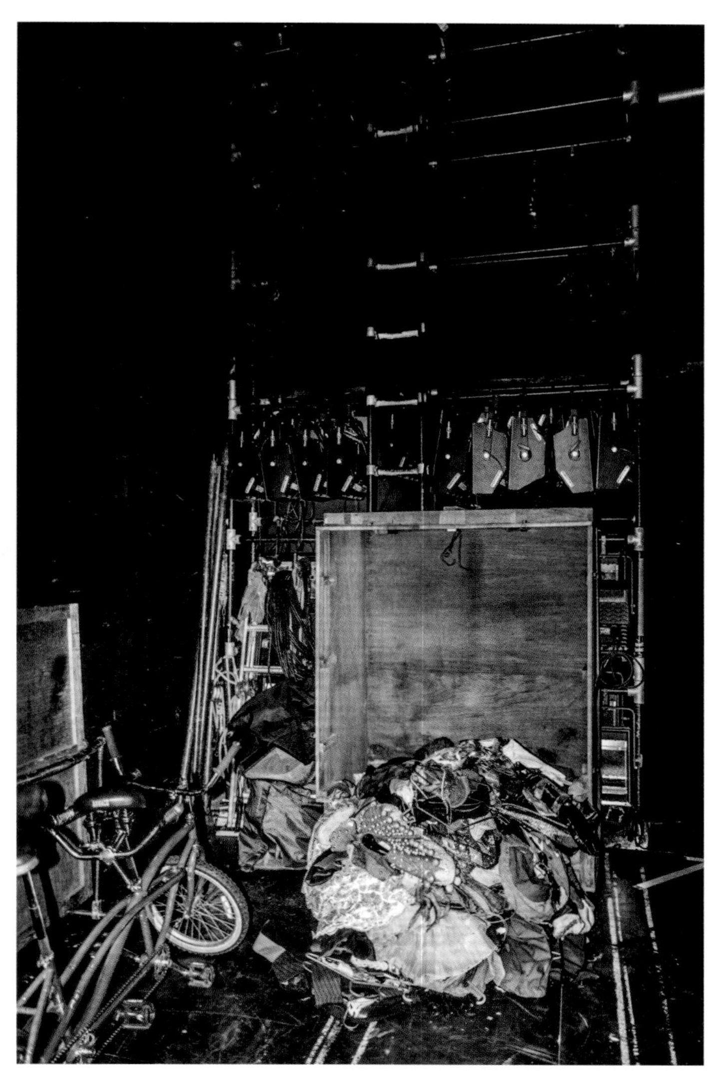

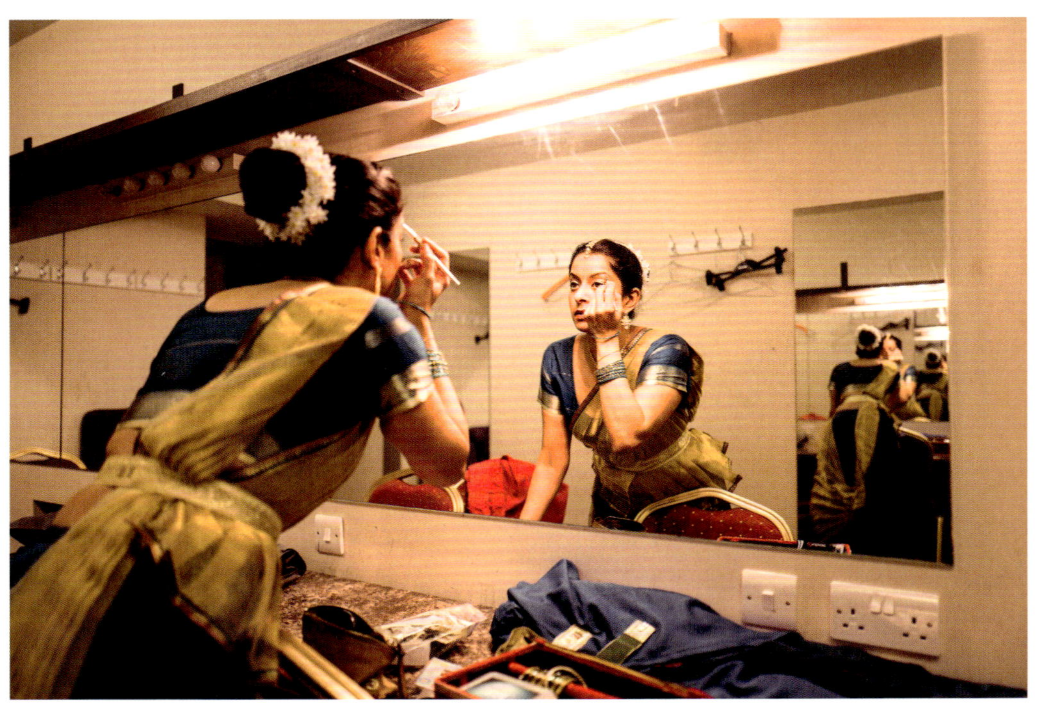

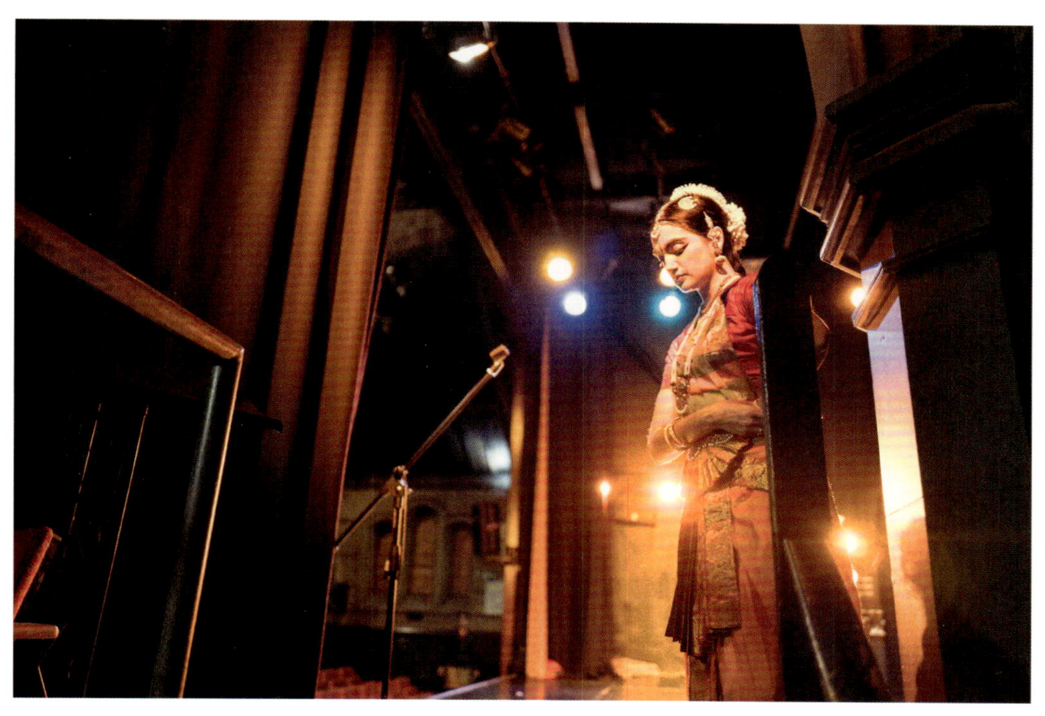

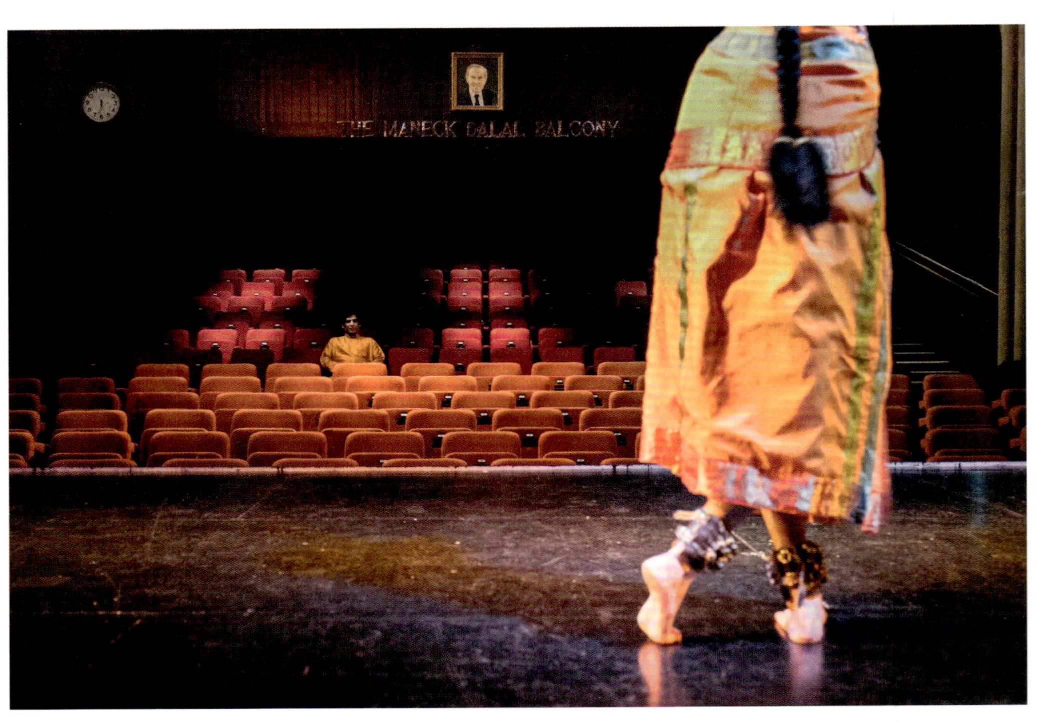
THE MANECK DALAL BALCONY

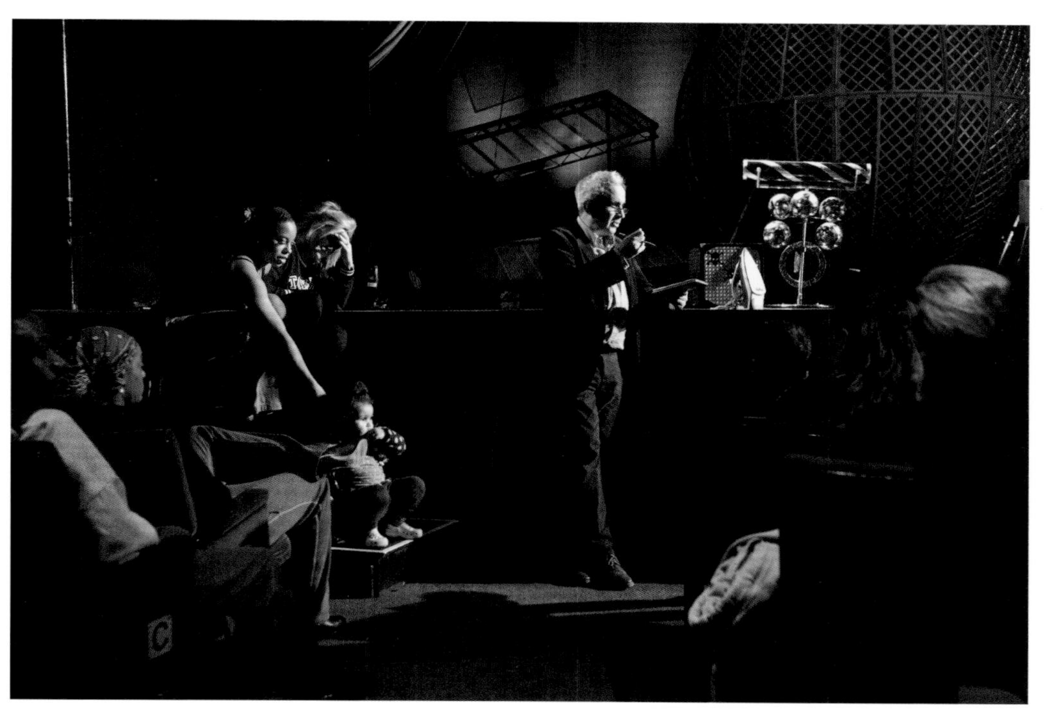

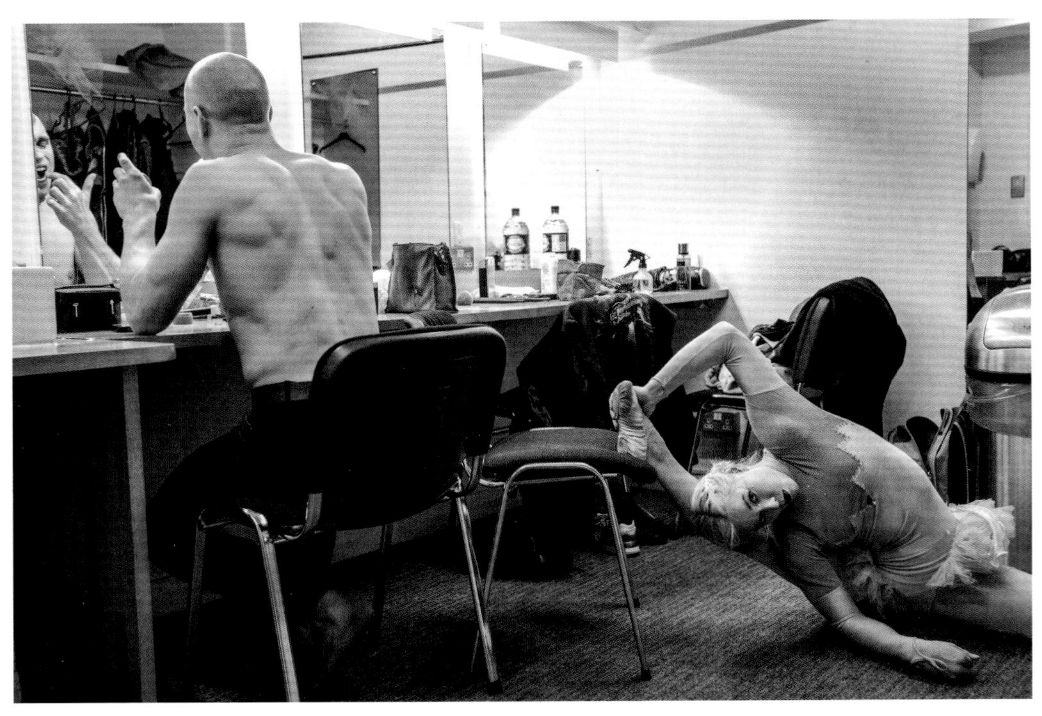

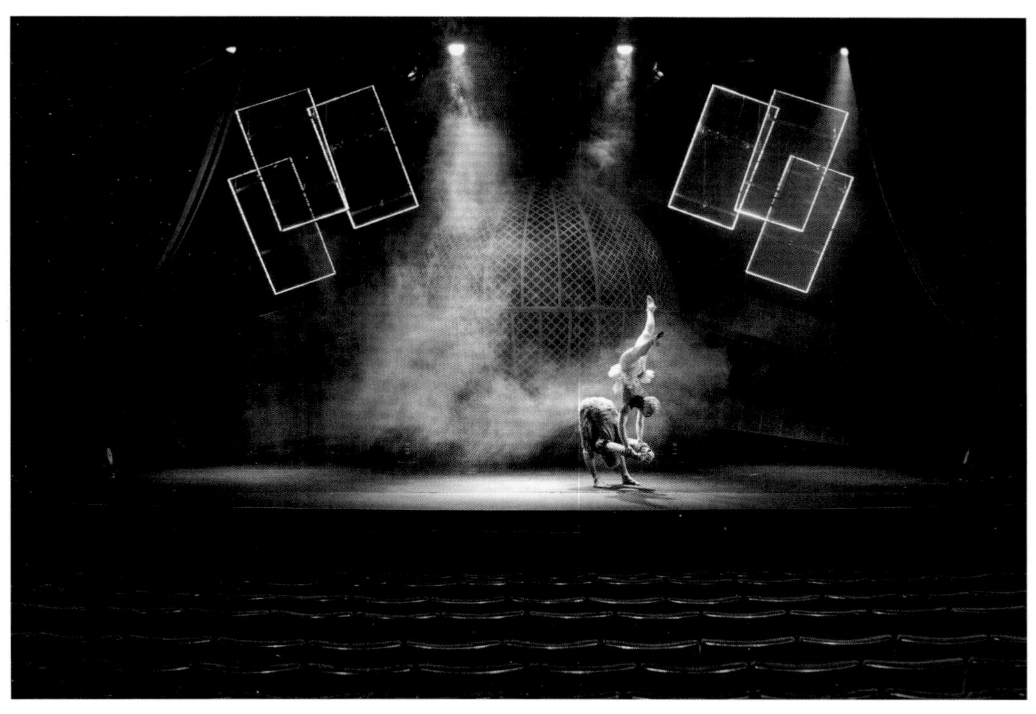

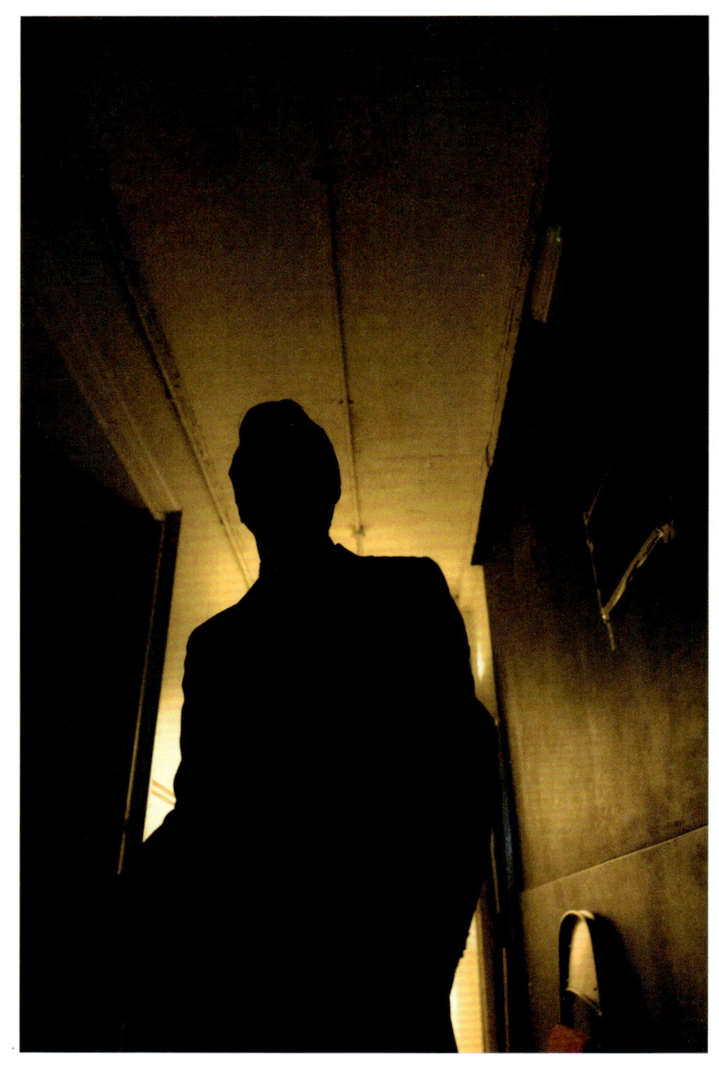

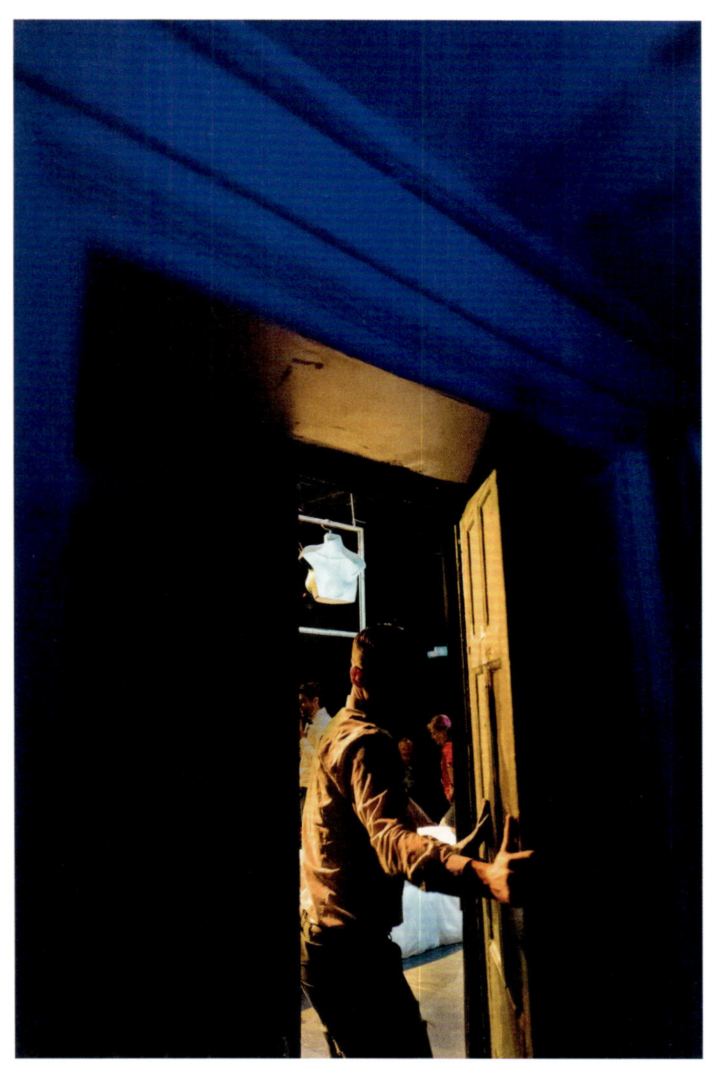

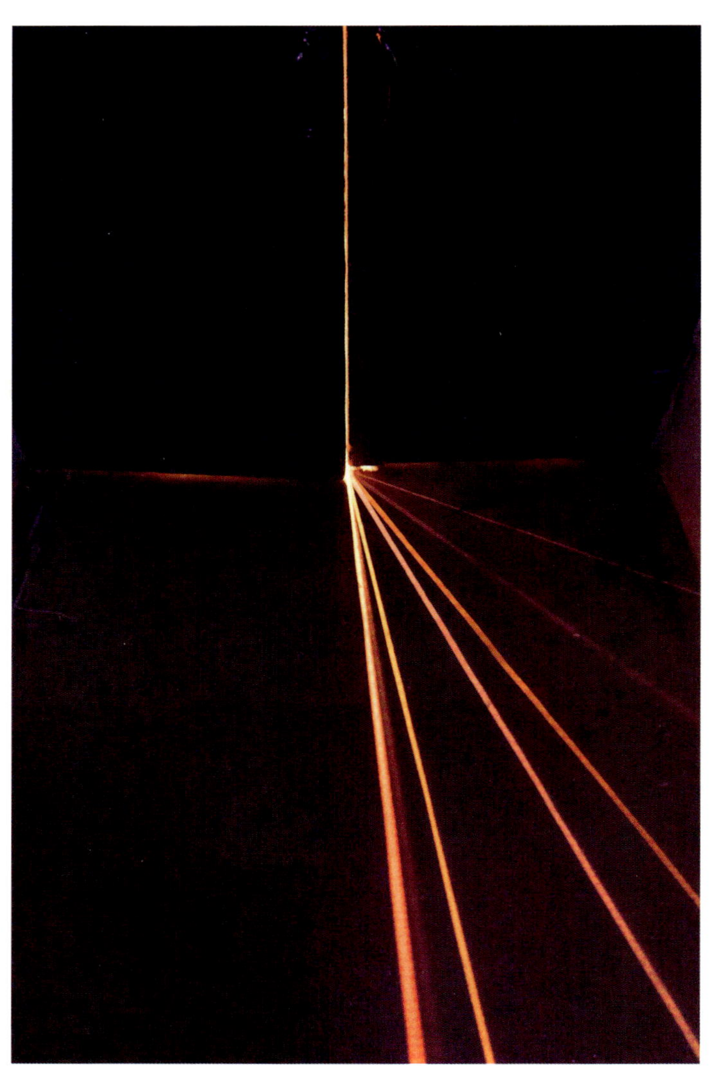

Marta Lallana García

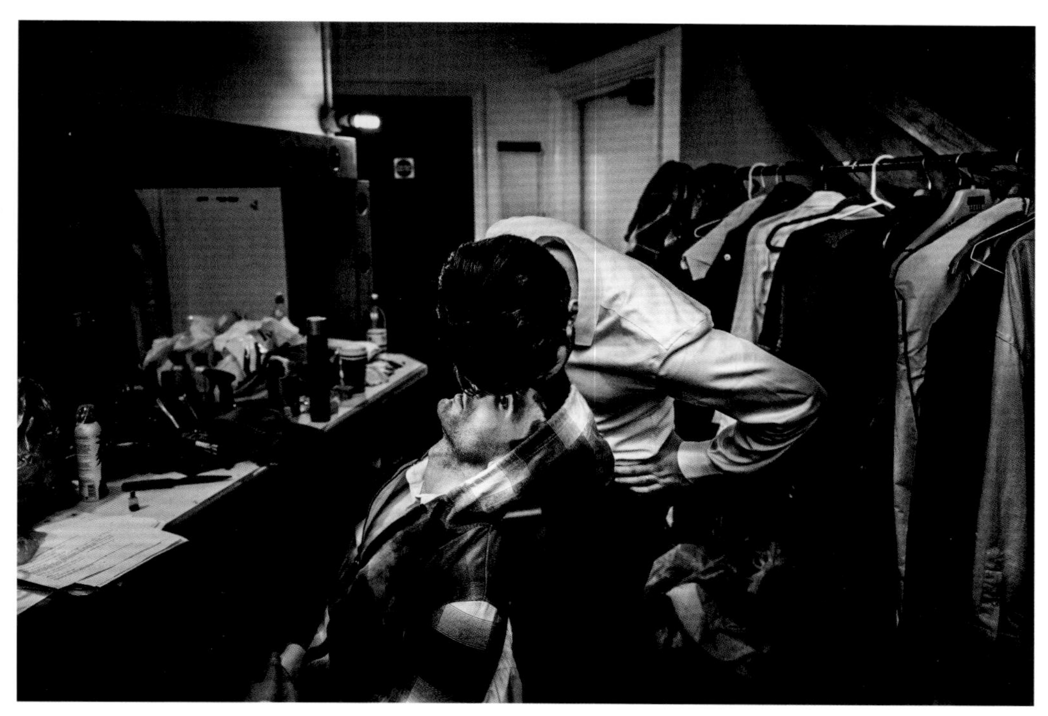

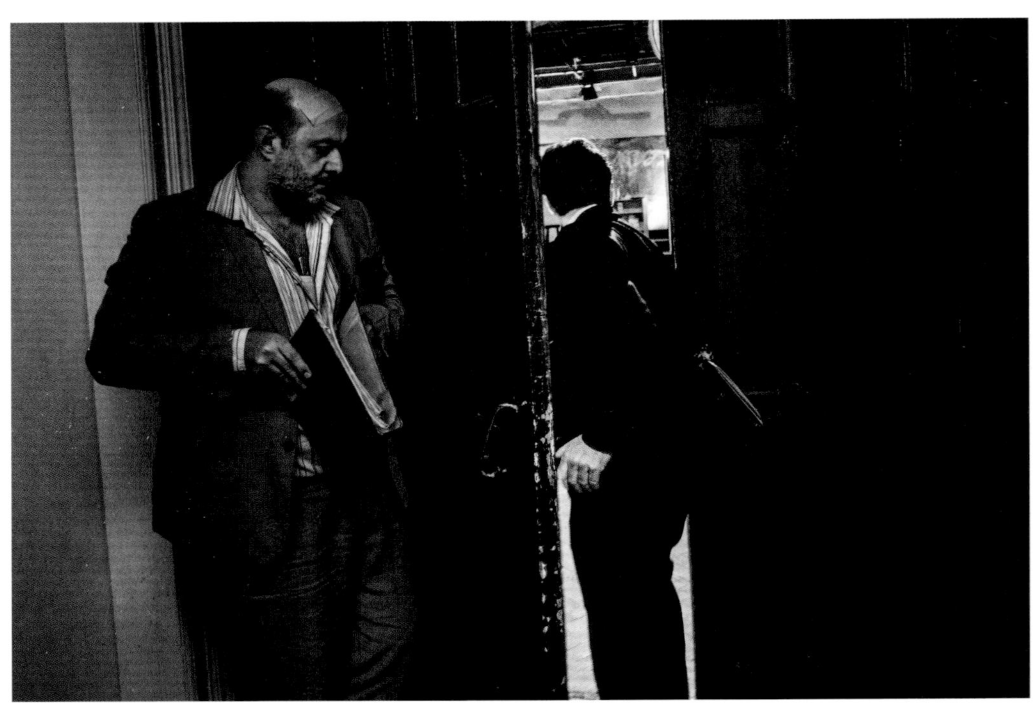

Yan Revazov

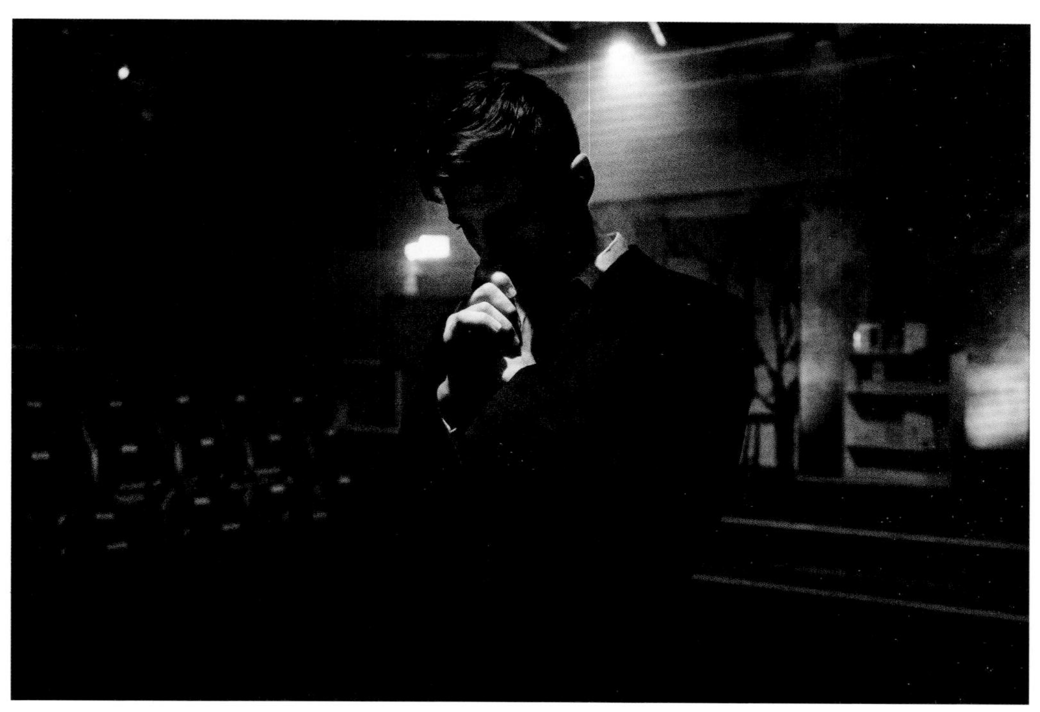

IRISH LANDSCAPE

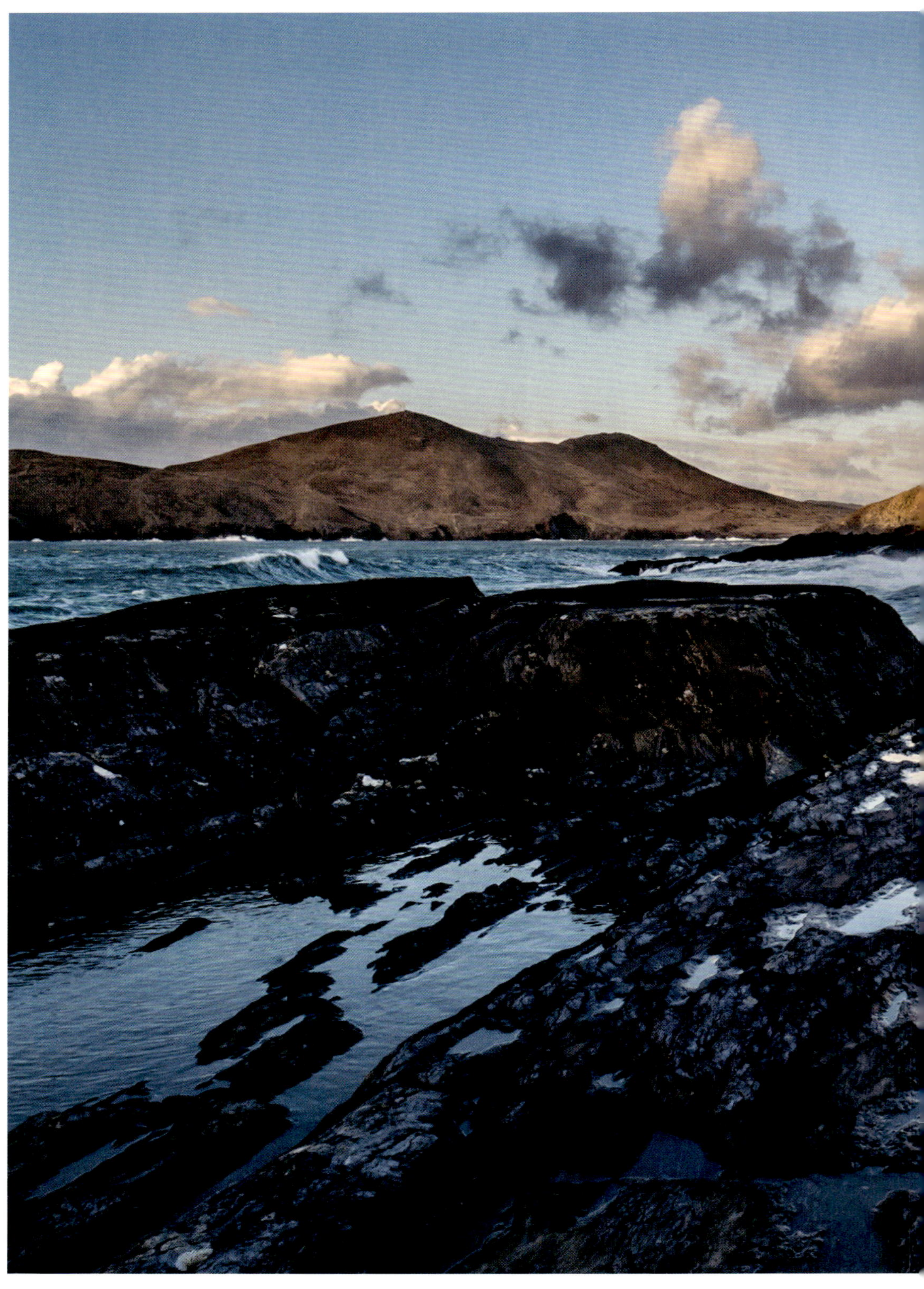

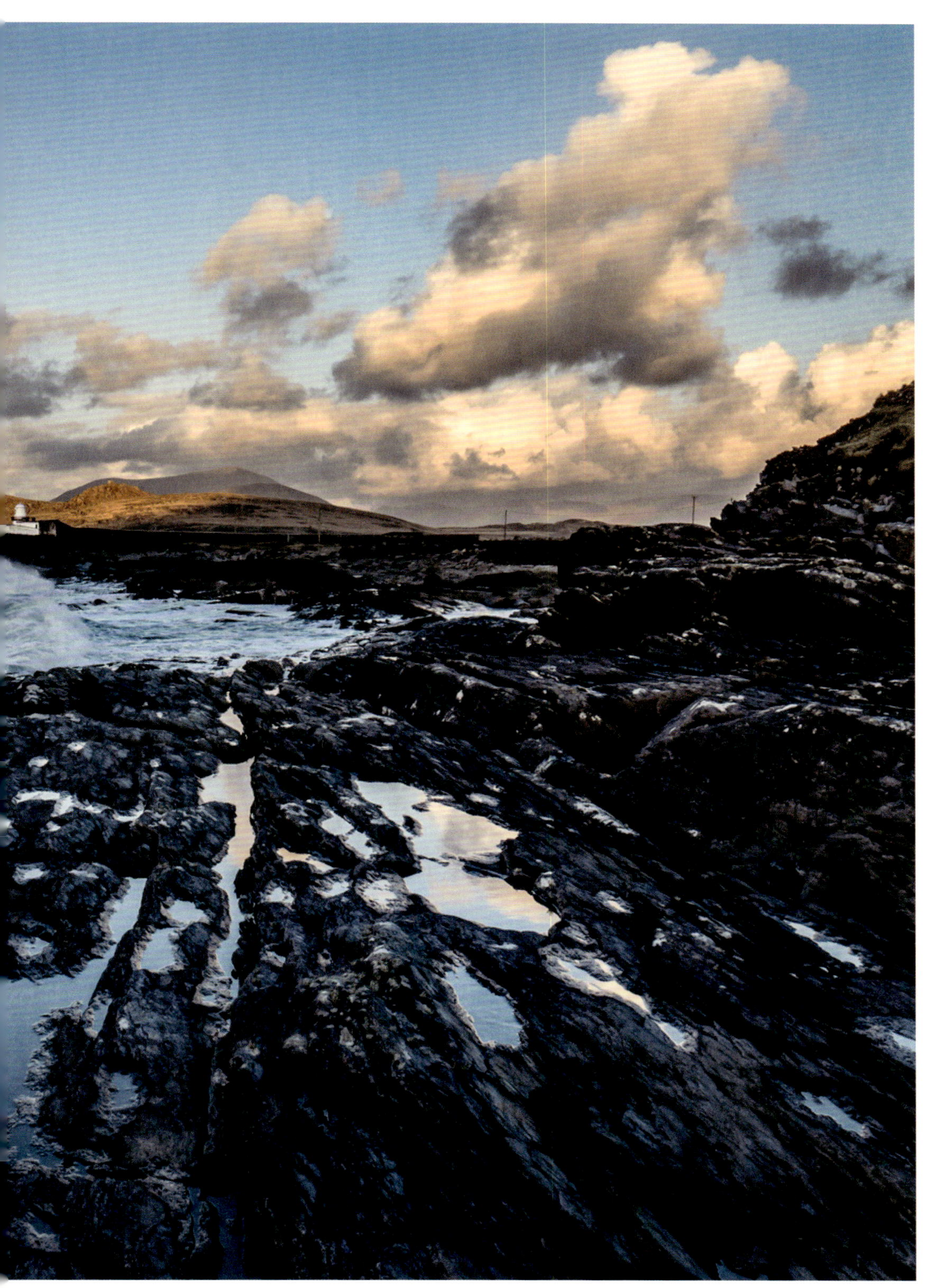

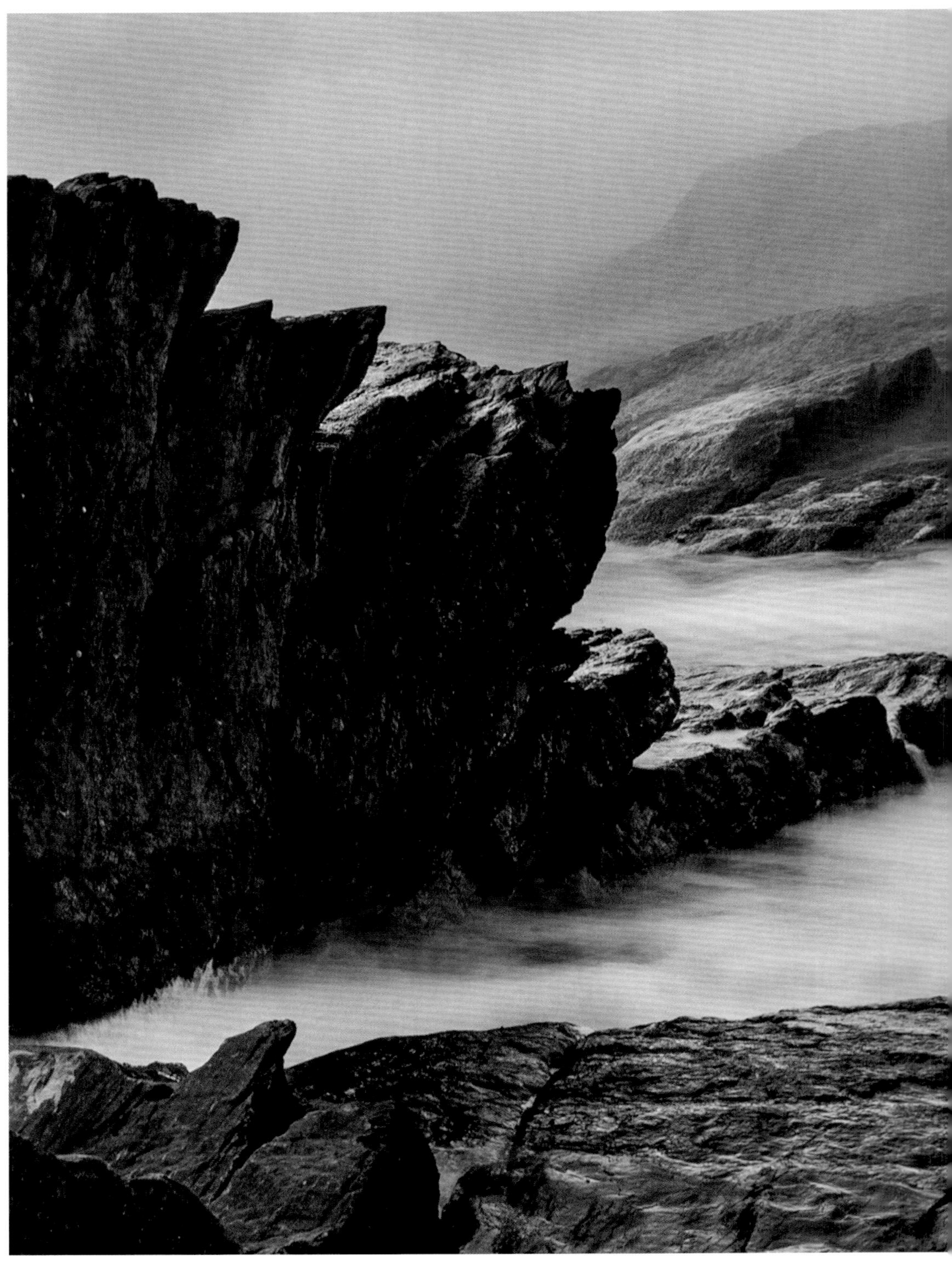

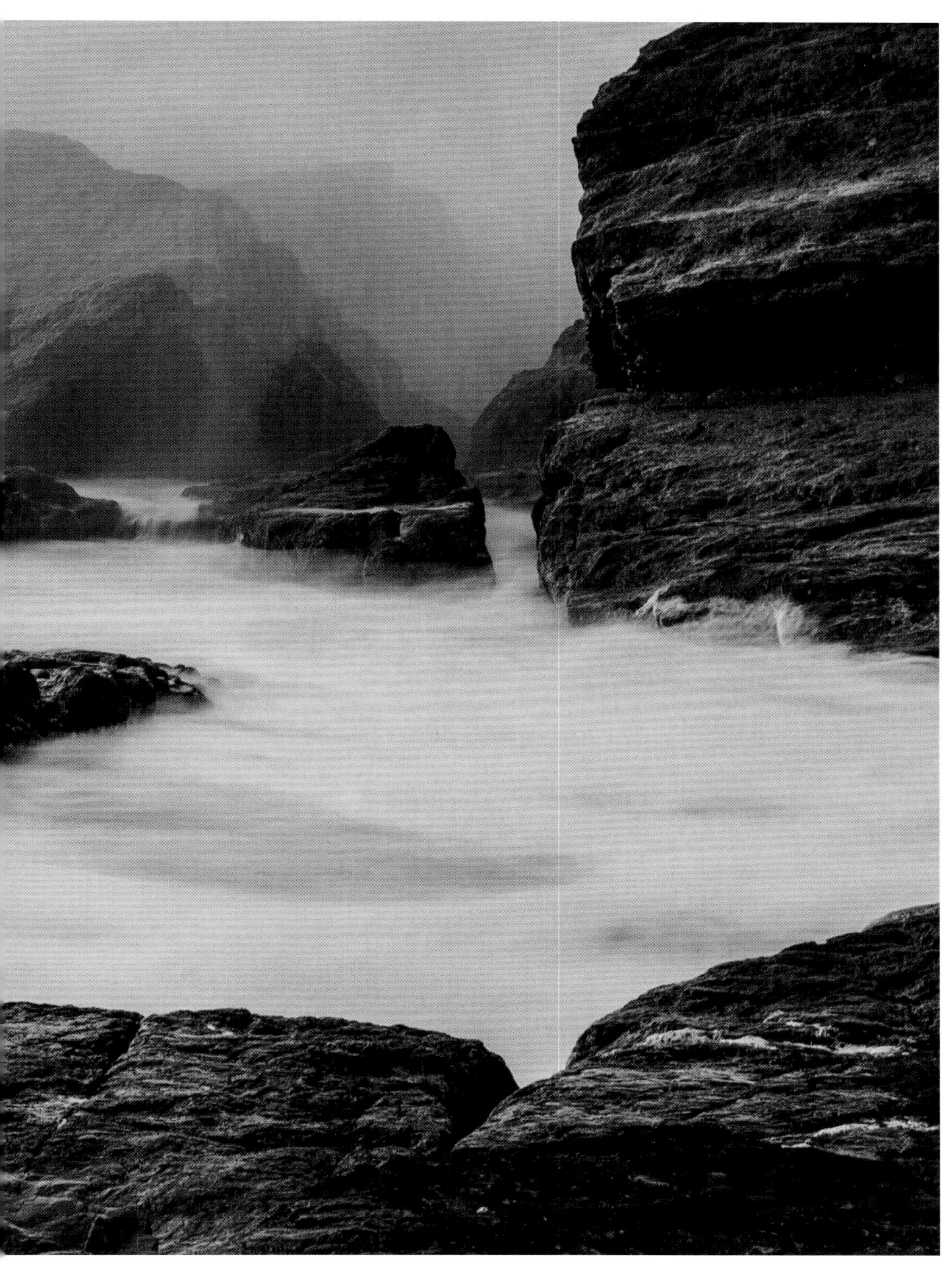

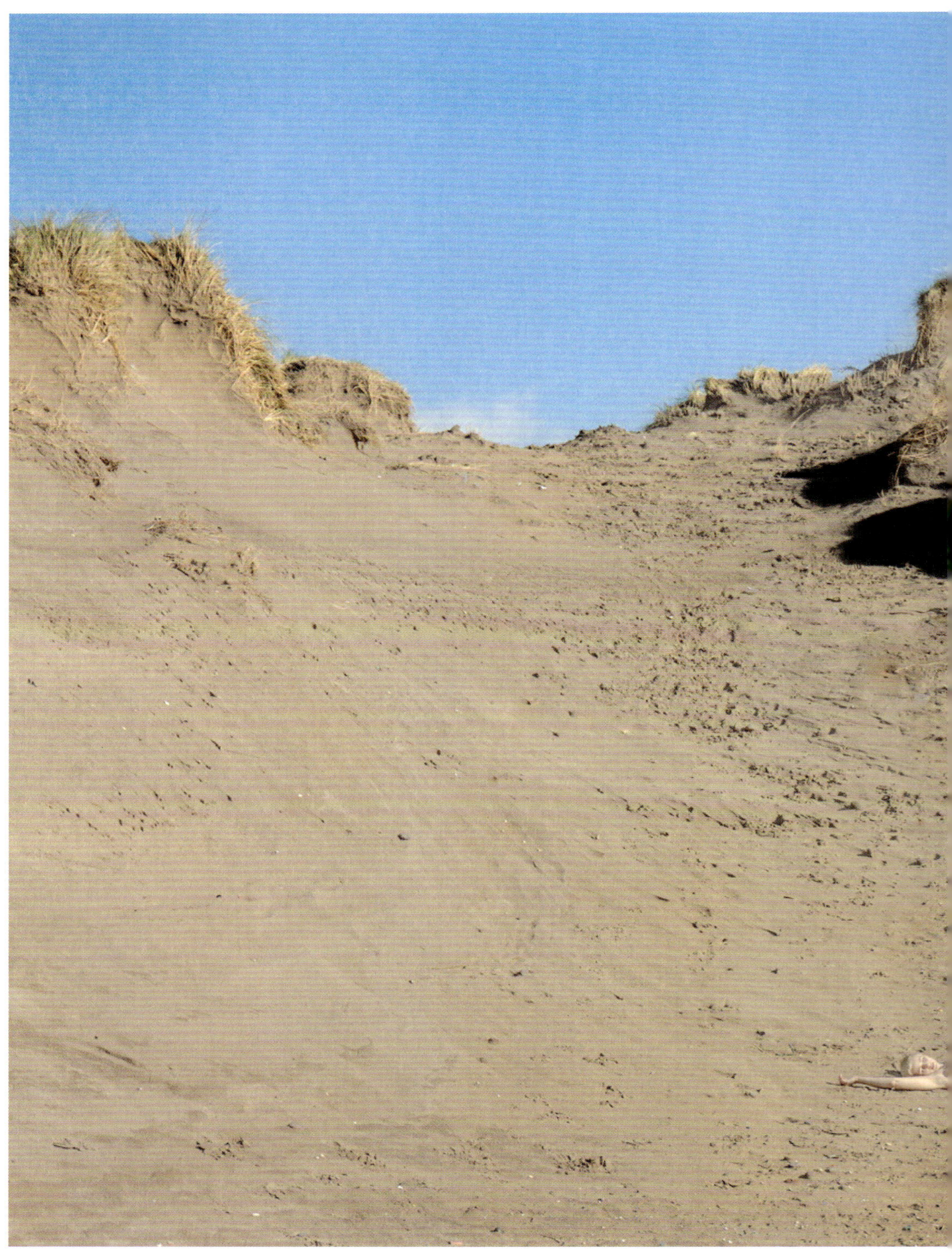

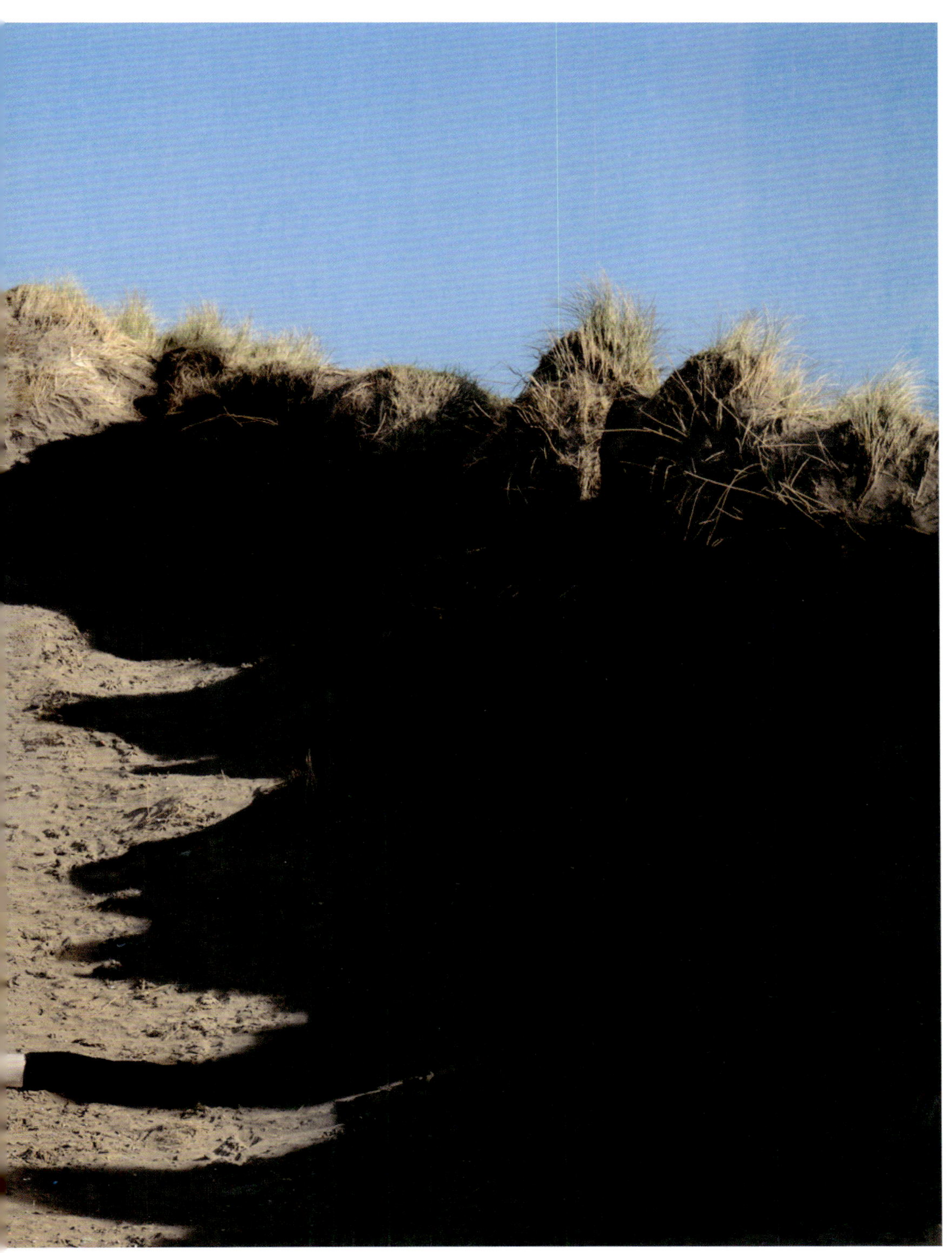

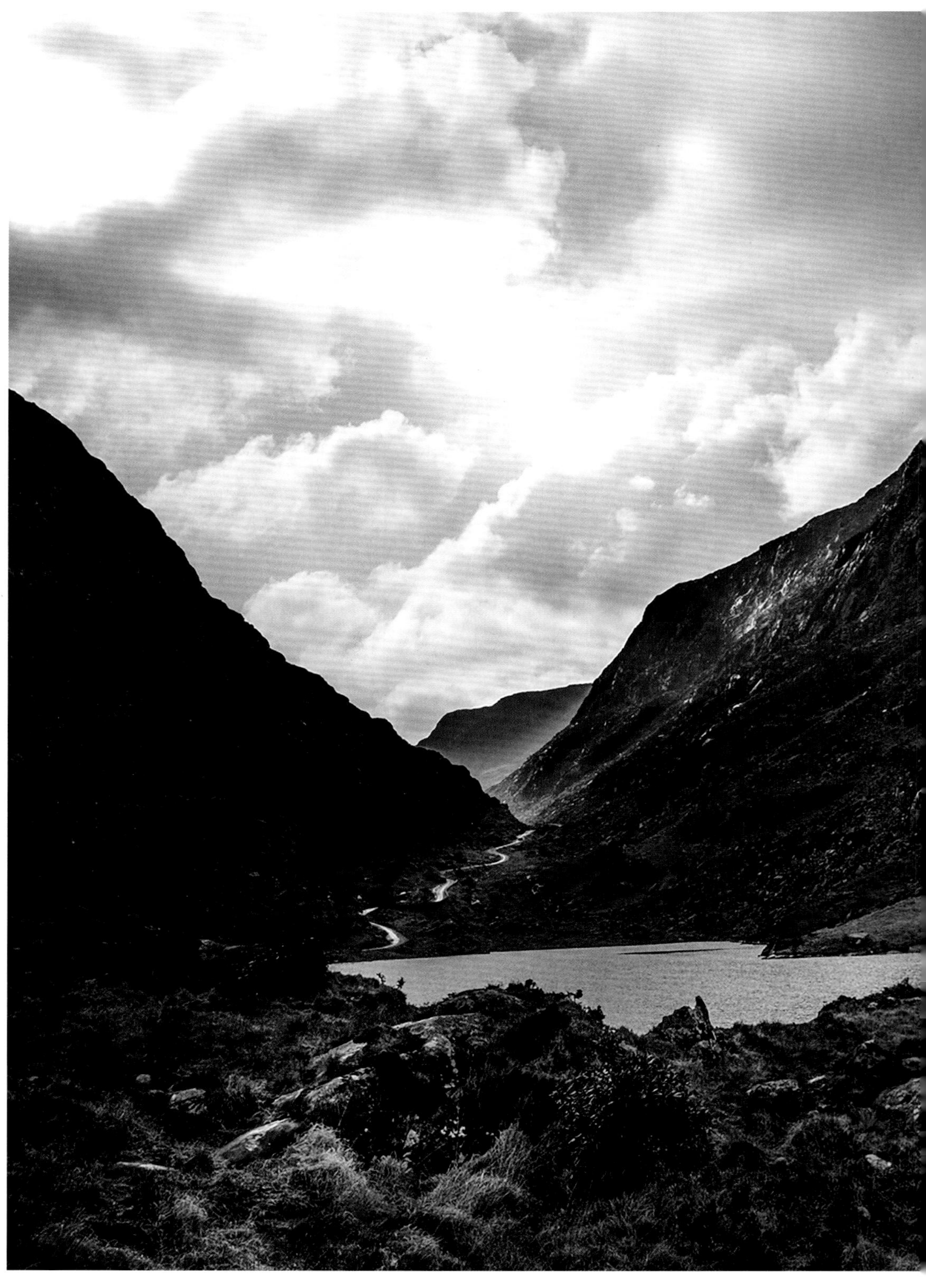

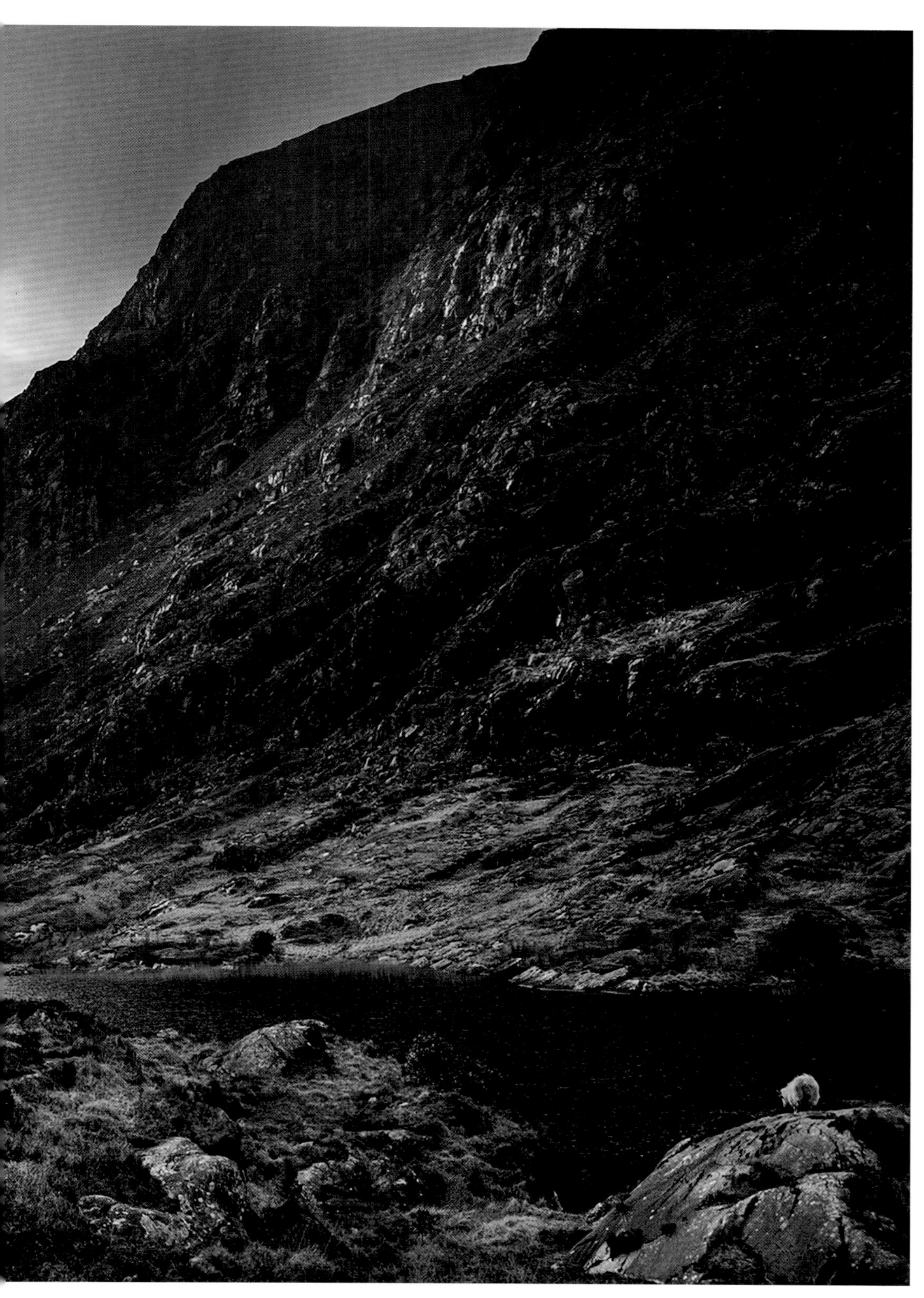

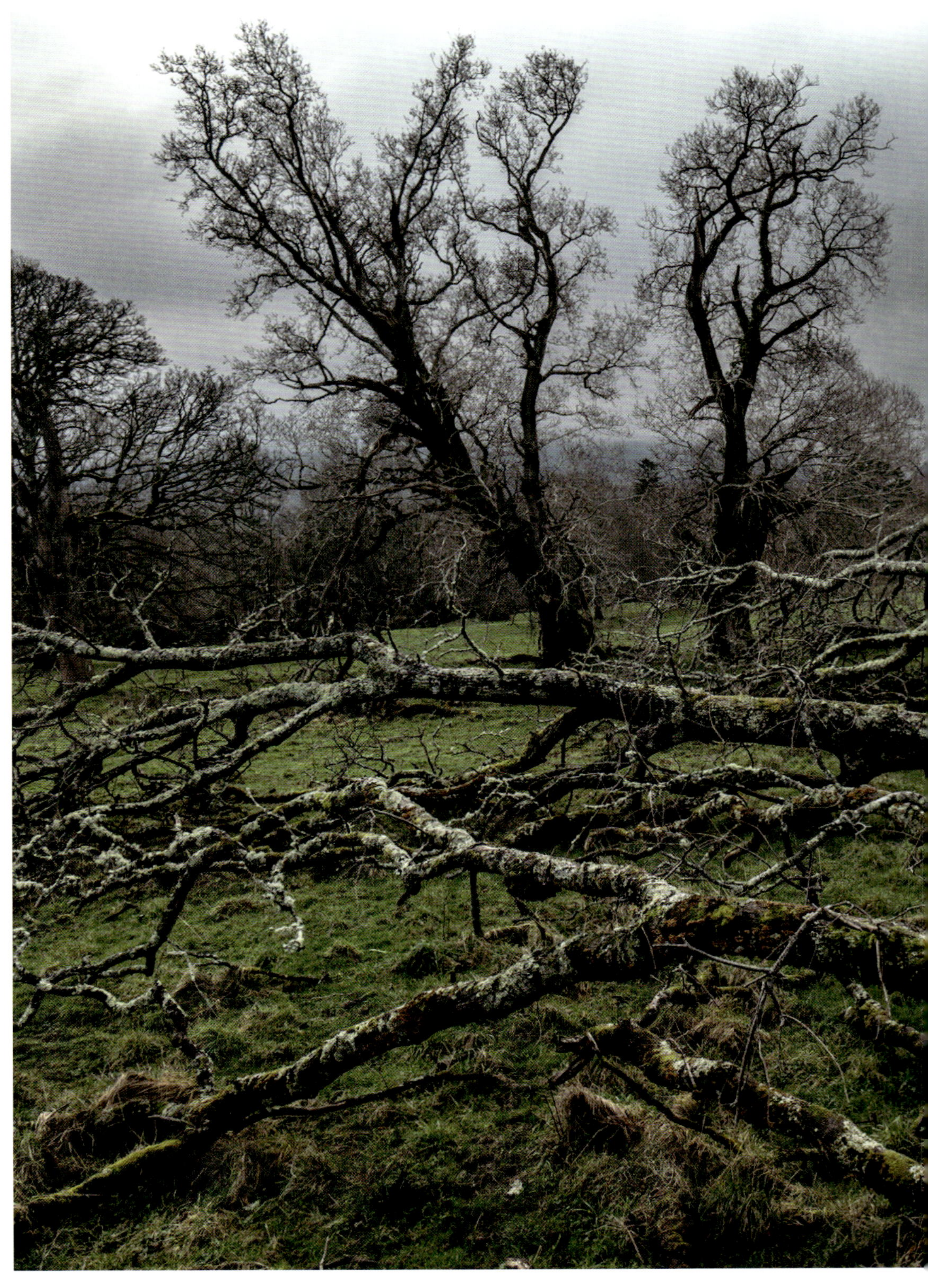

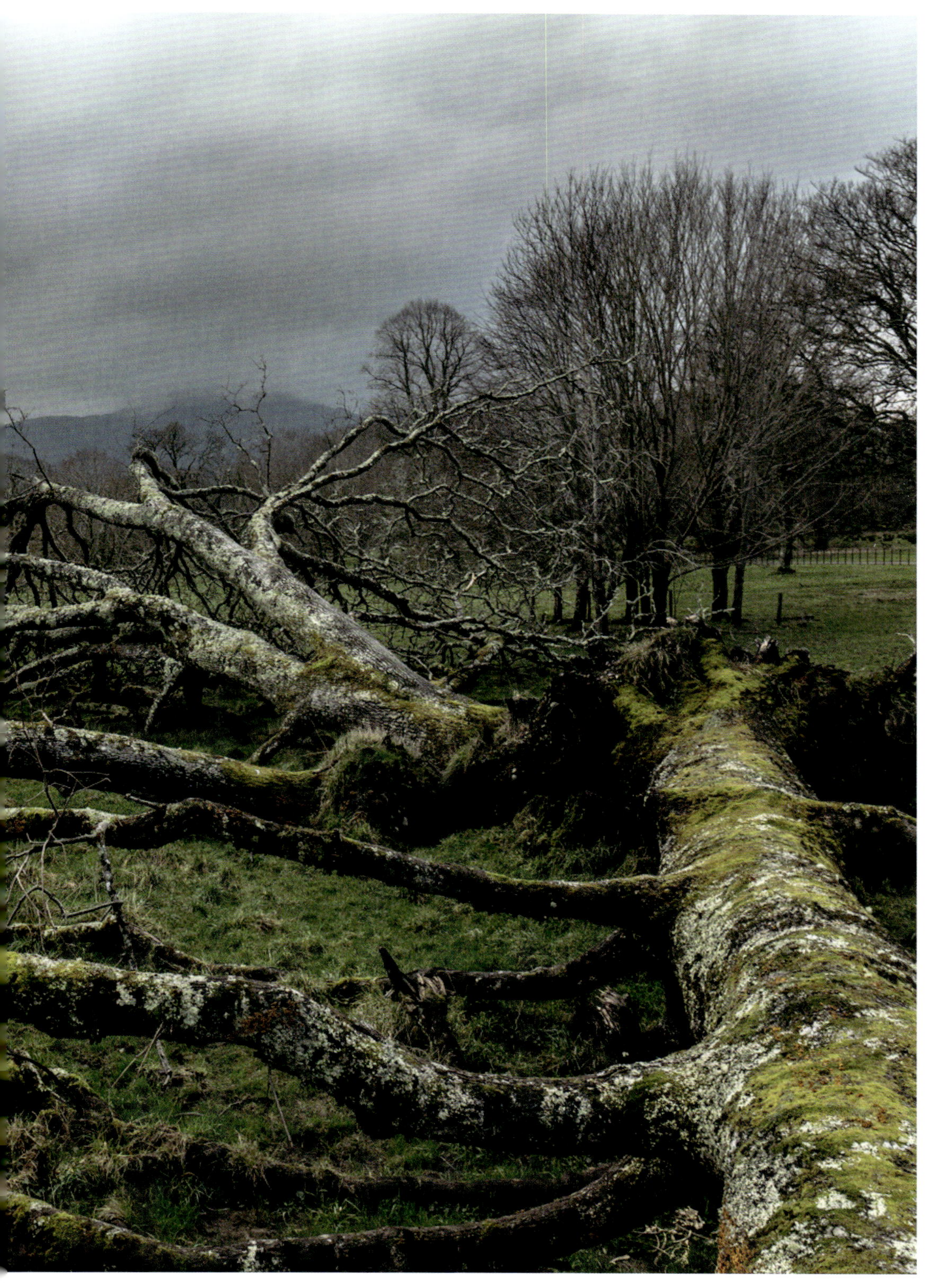

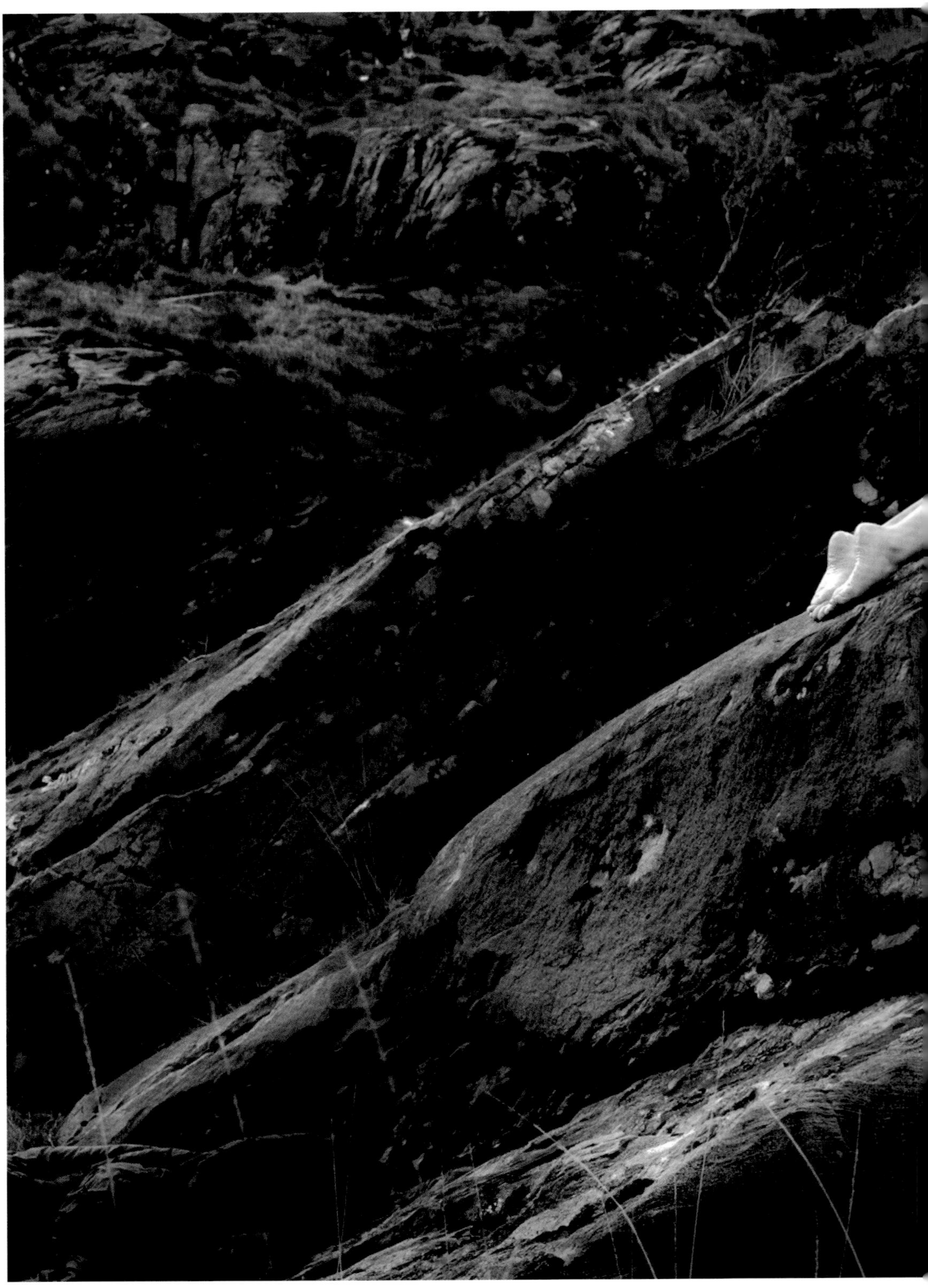

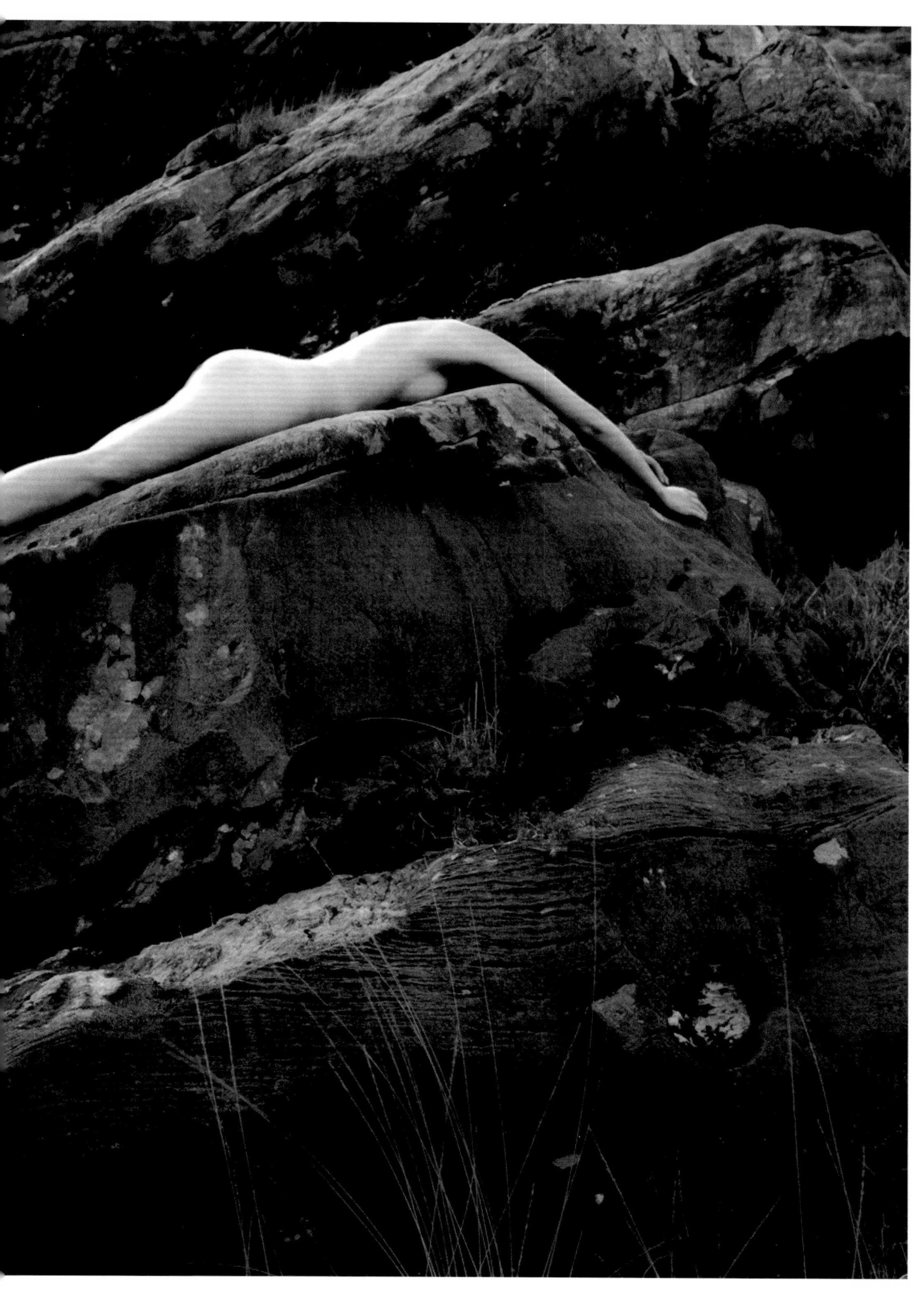

HOME SWEET HOME

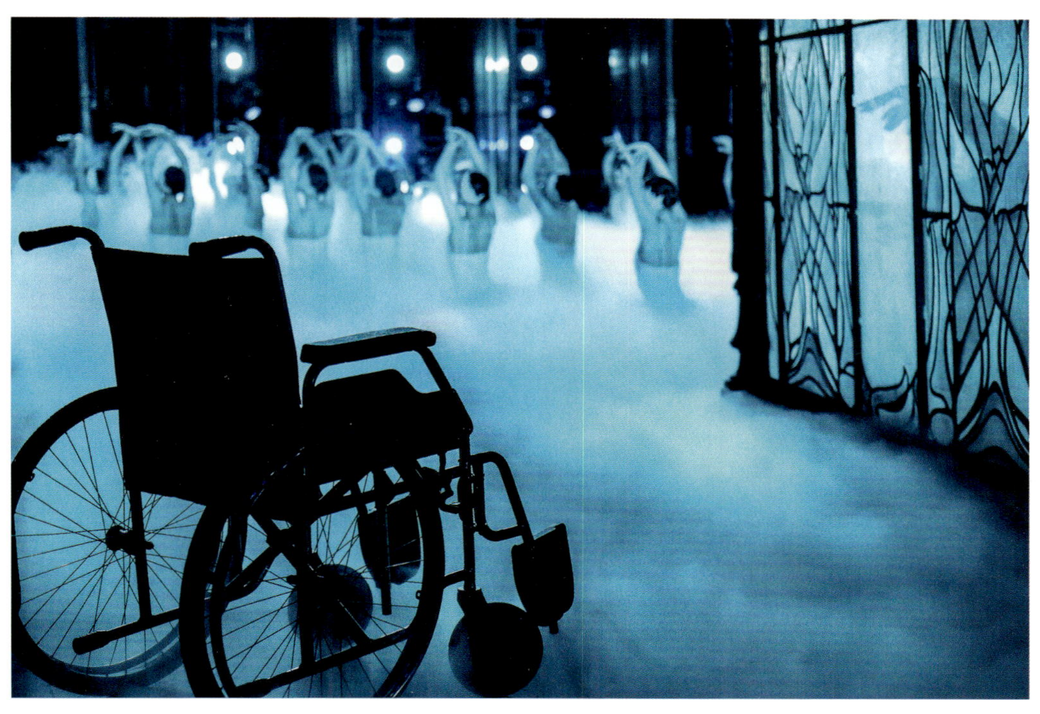

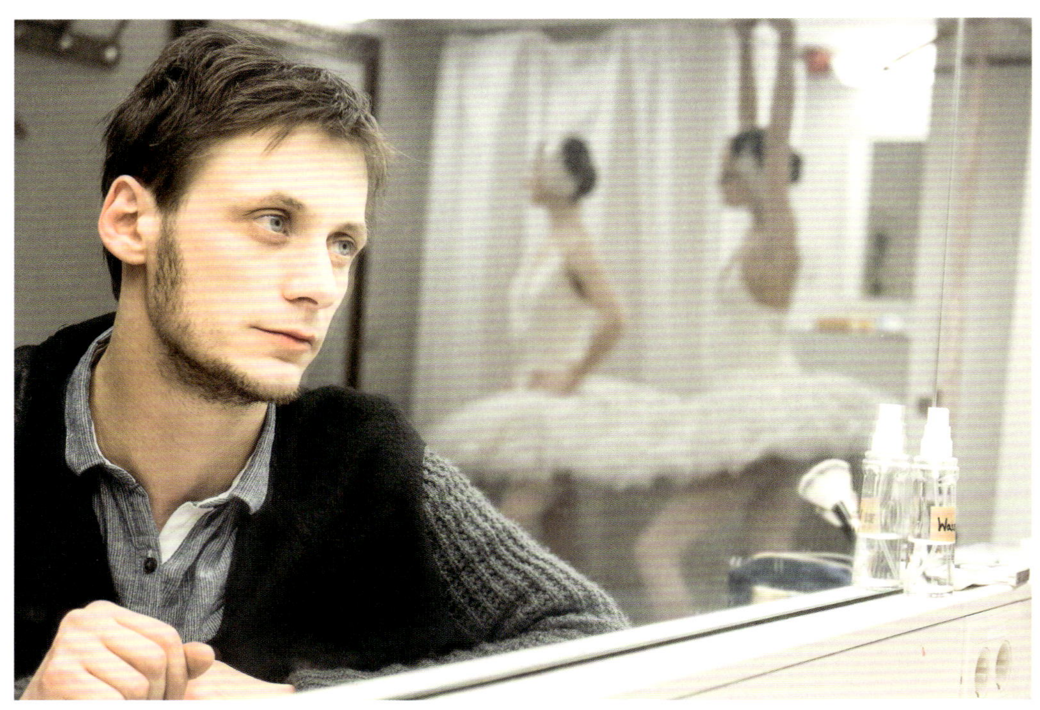

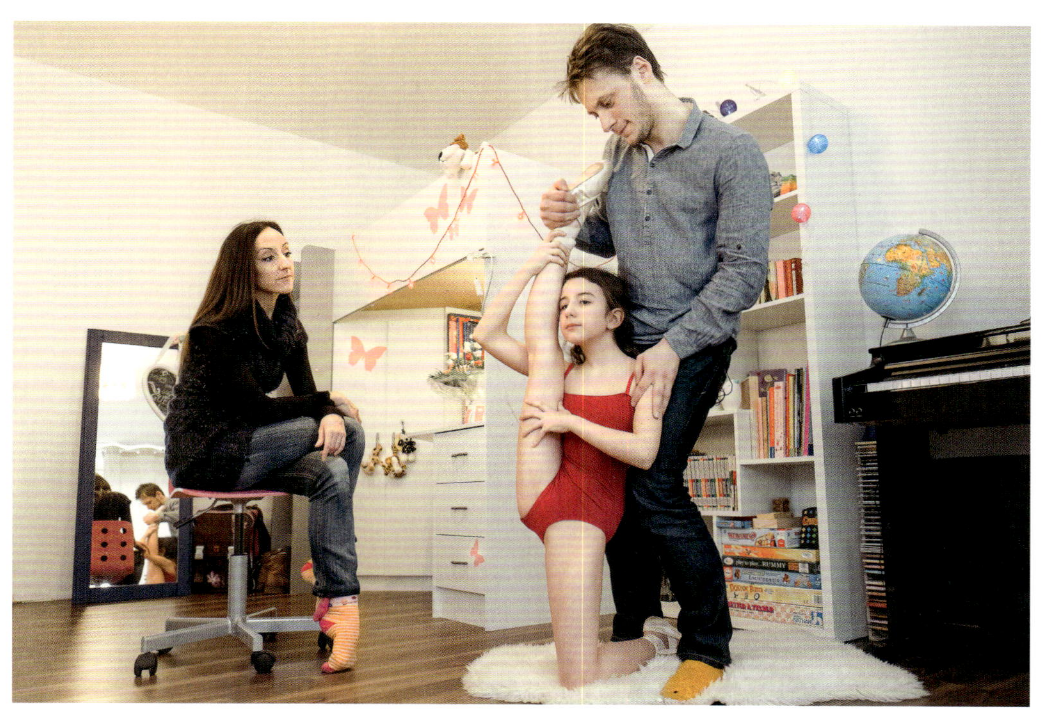

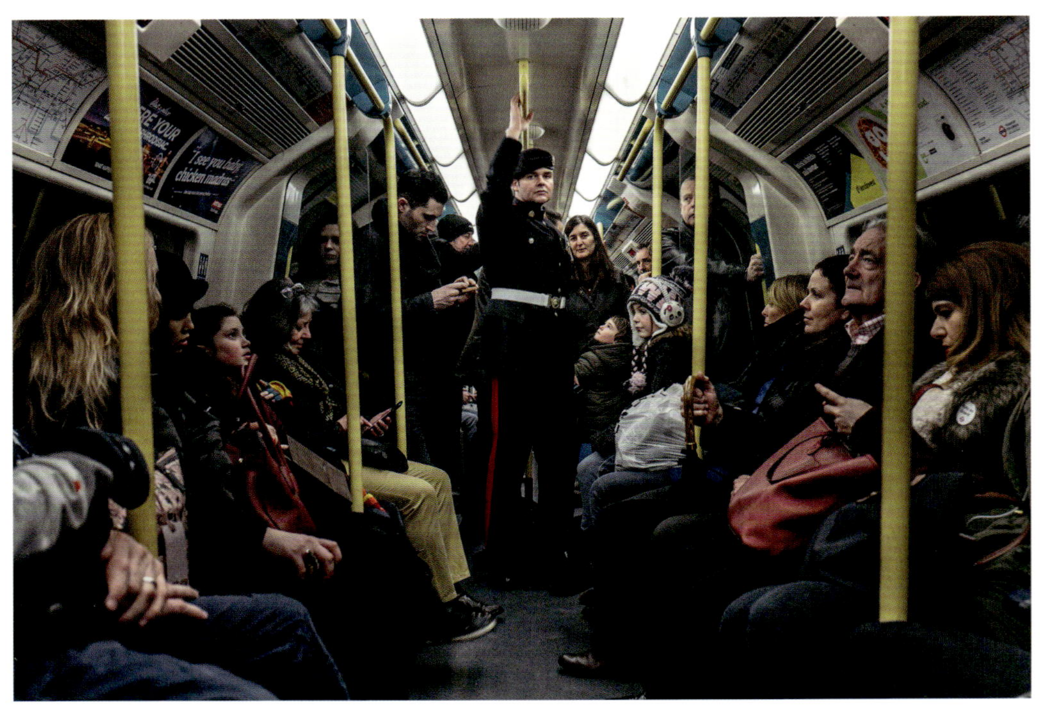

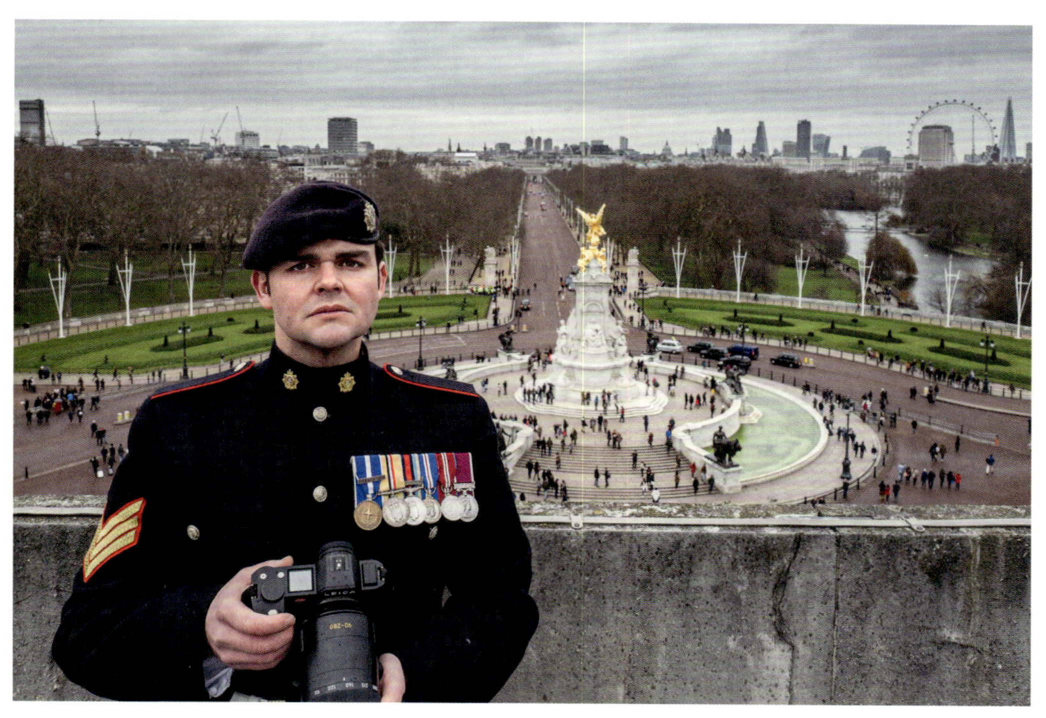

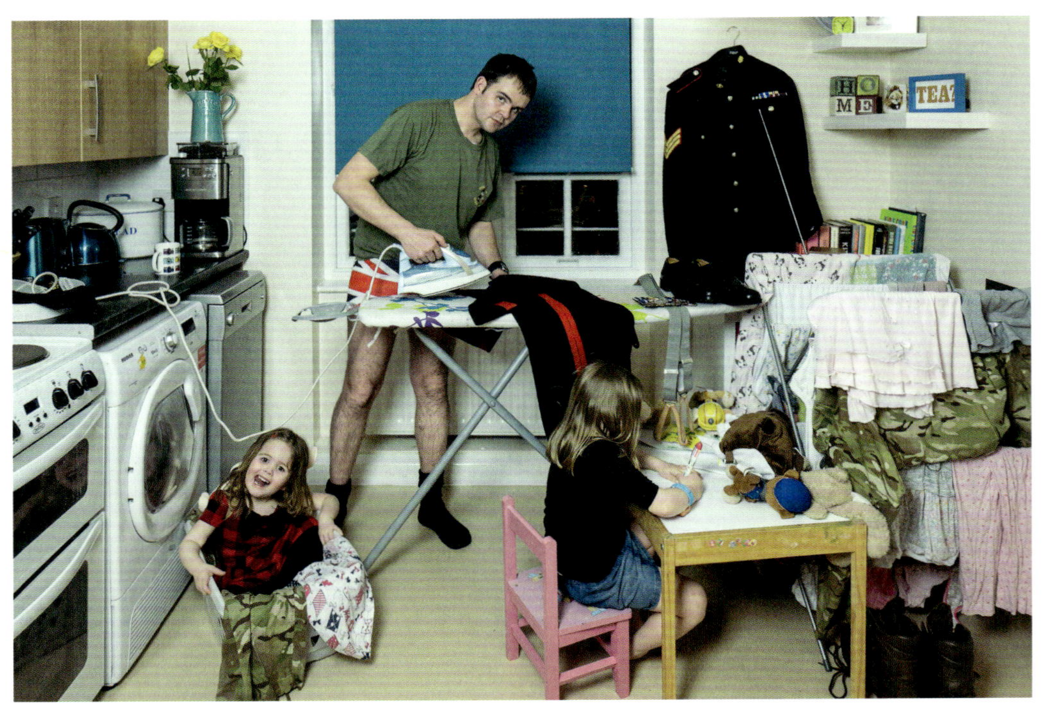

Rupert Frere

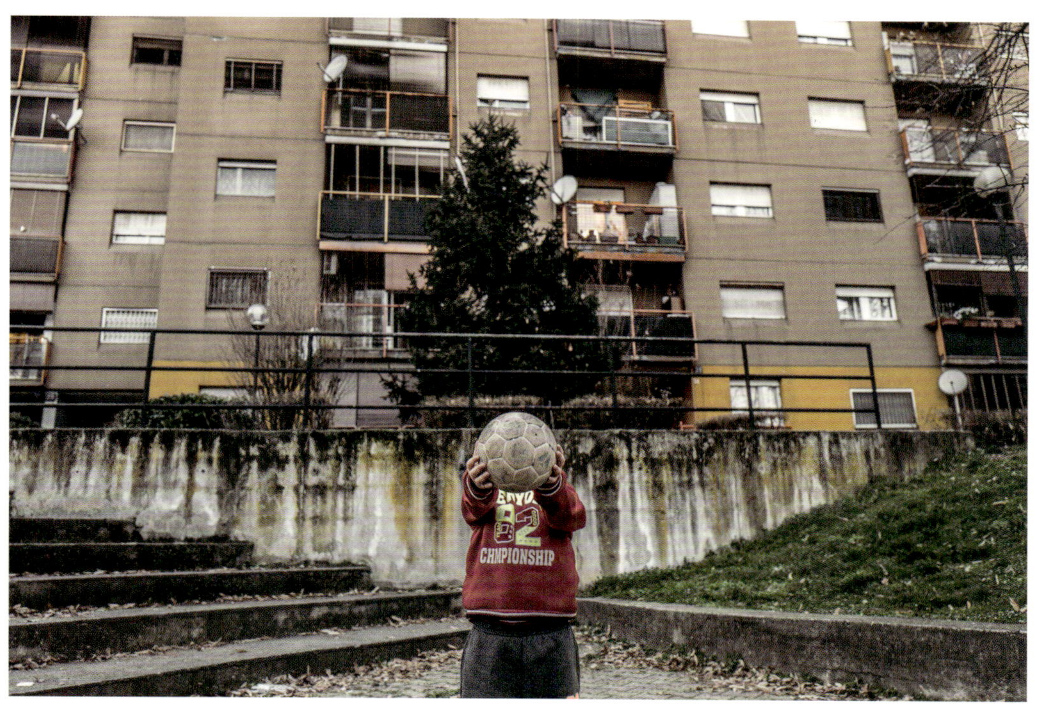
82
CHMPIONSHIP

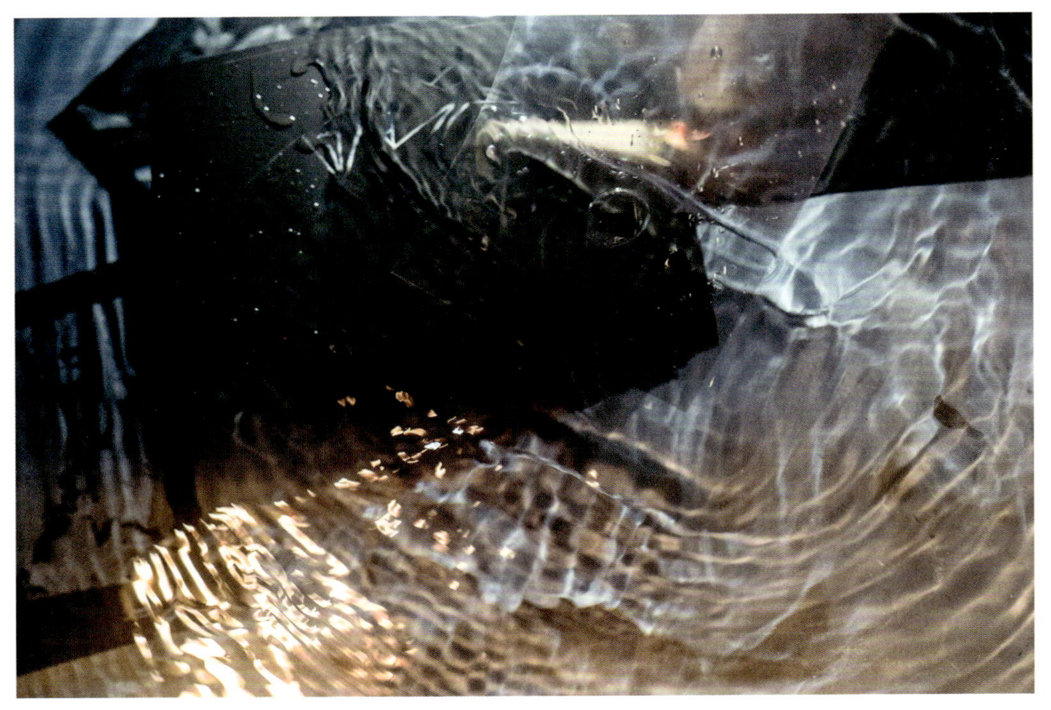

Gabriele Micalizzi

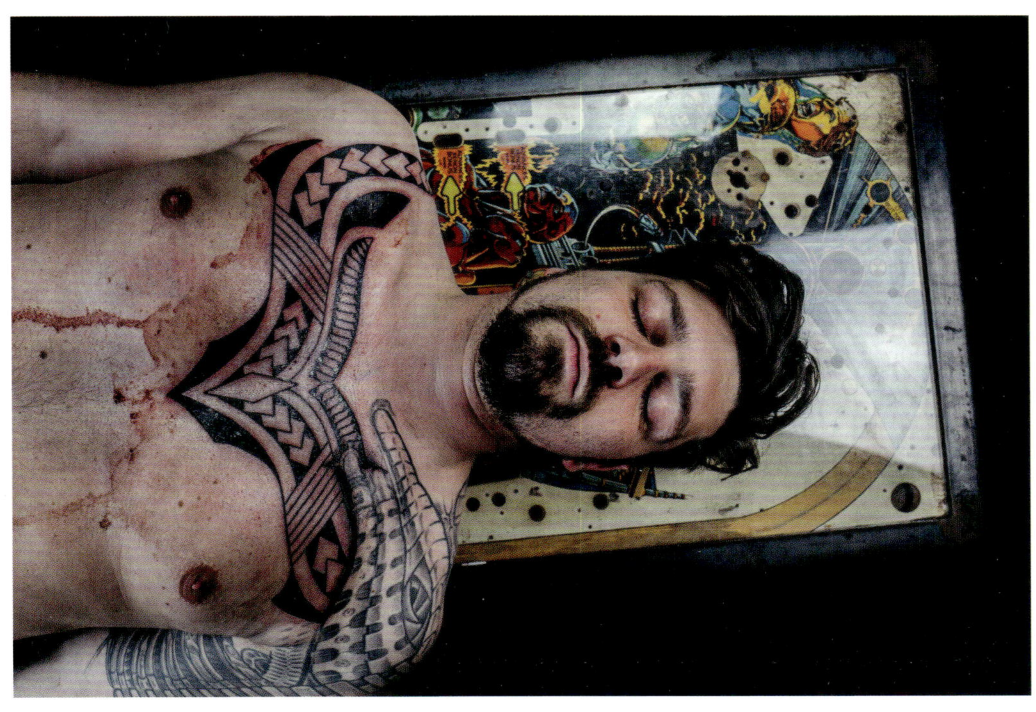

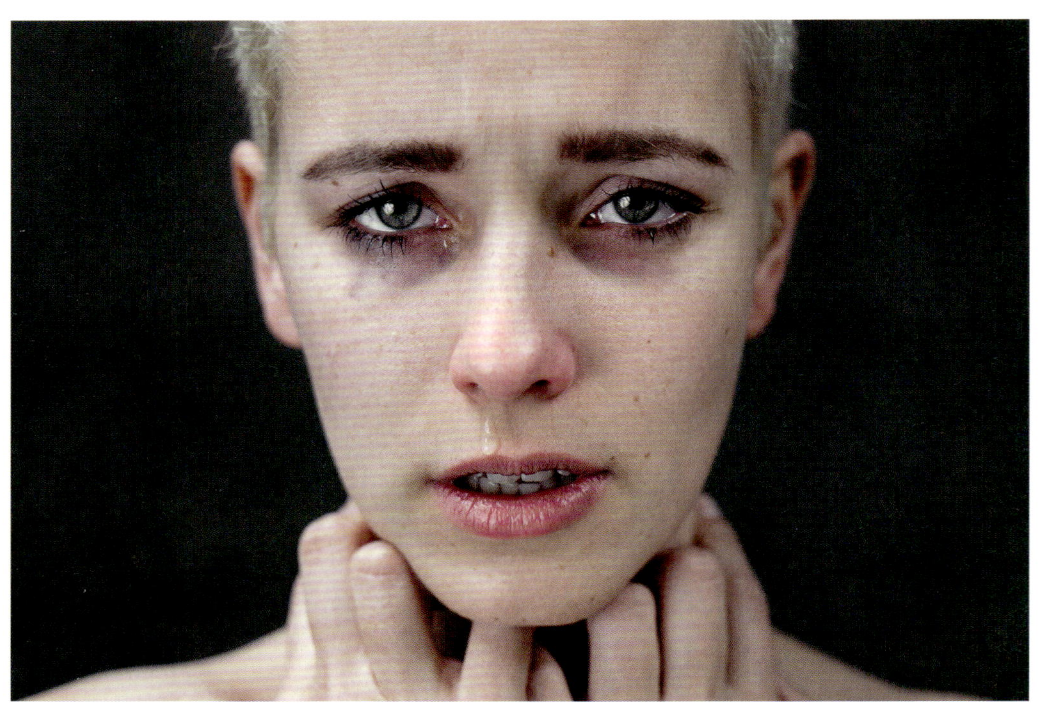

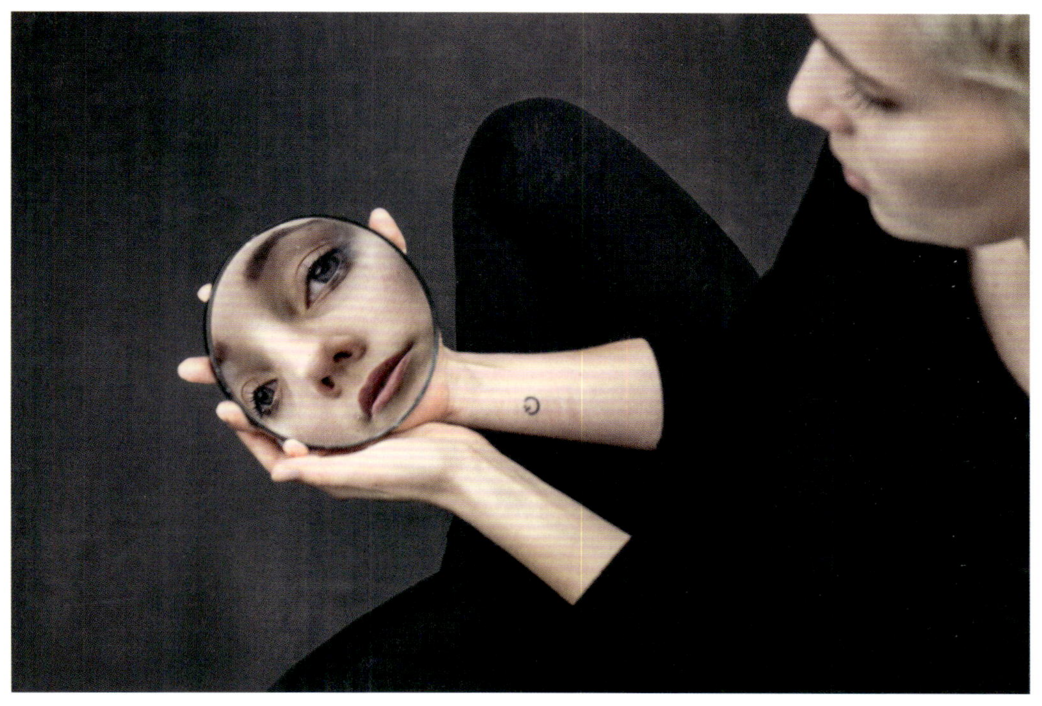

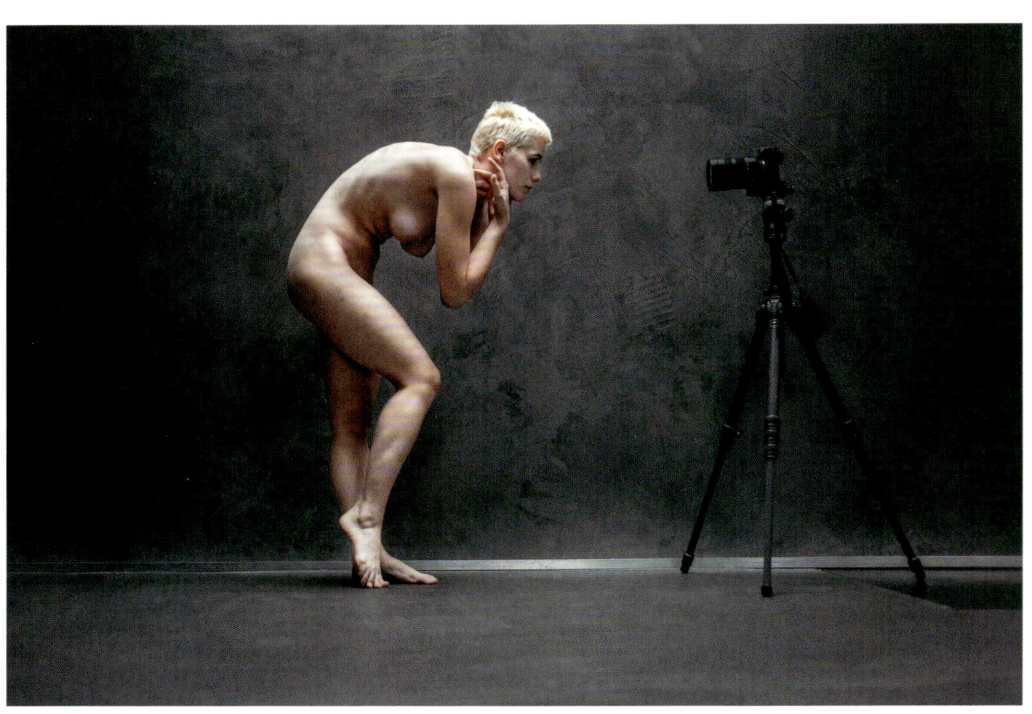

Laura Zalenga

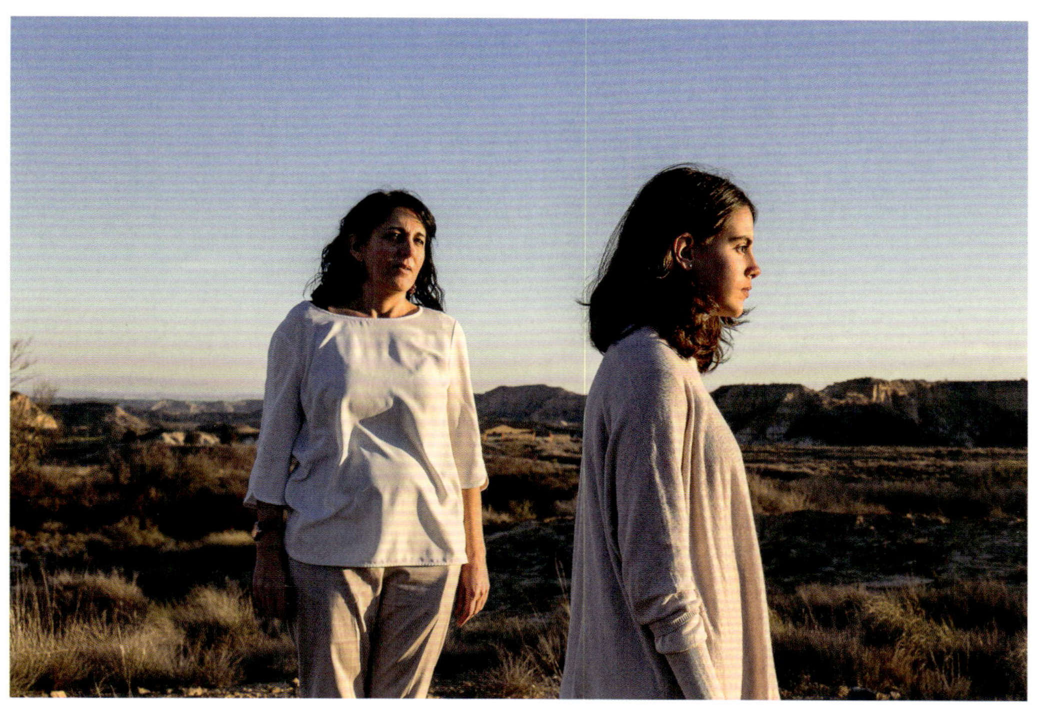

Marta Lallana García

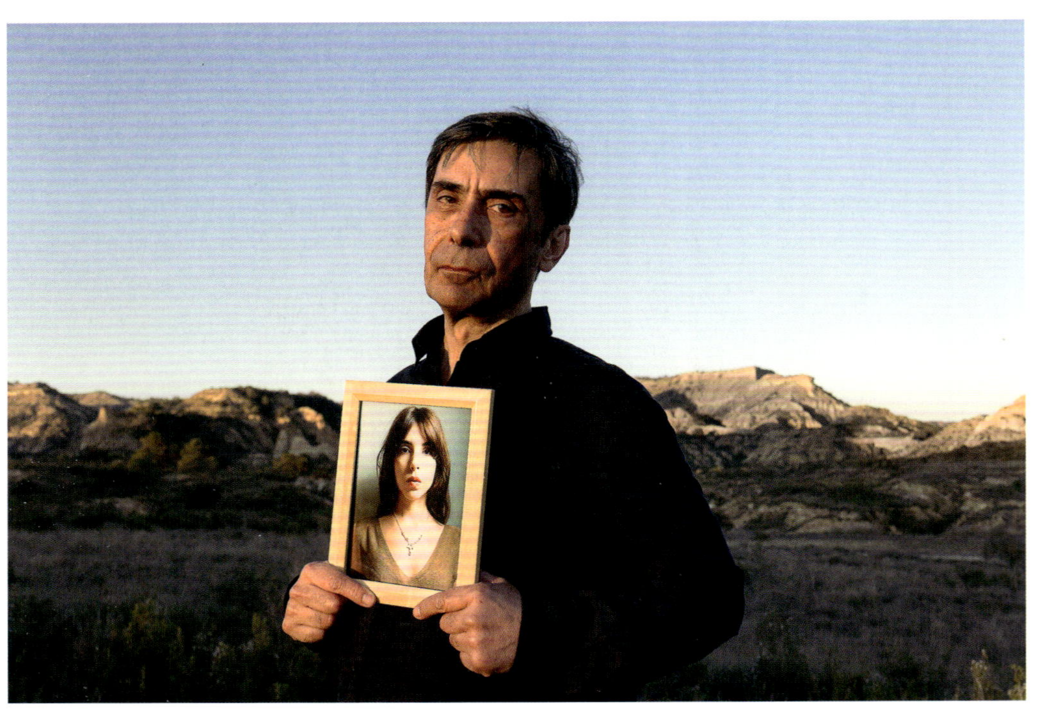

Marta Lallana García

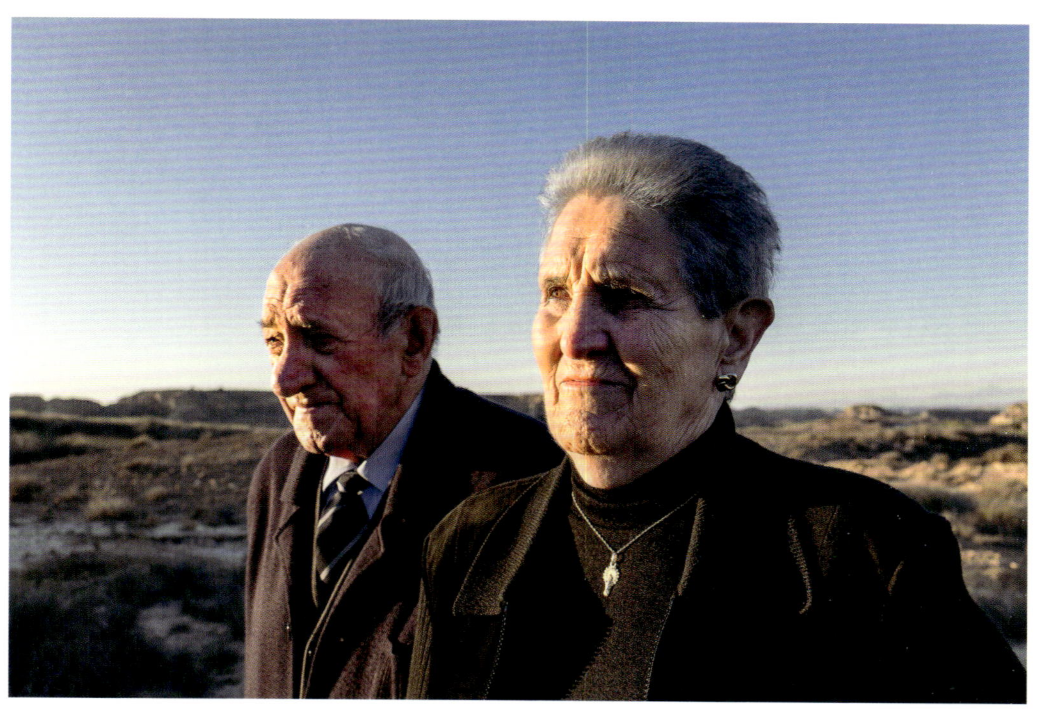

Marta Lallana García

PLACES AND FACES

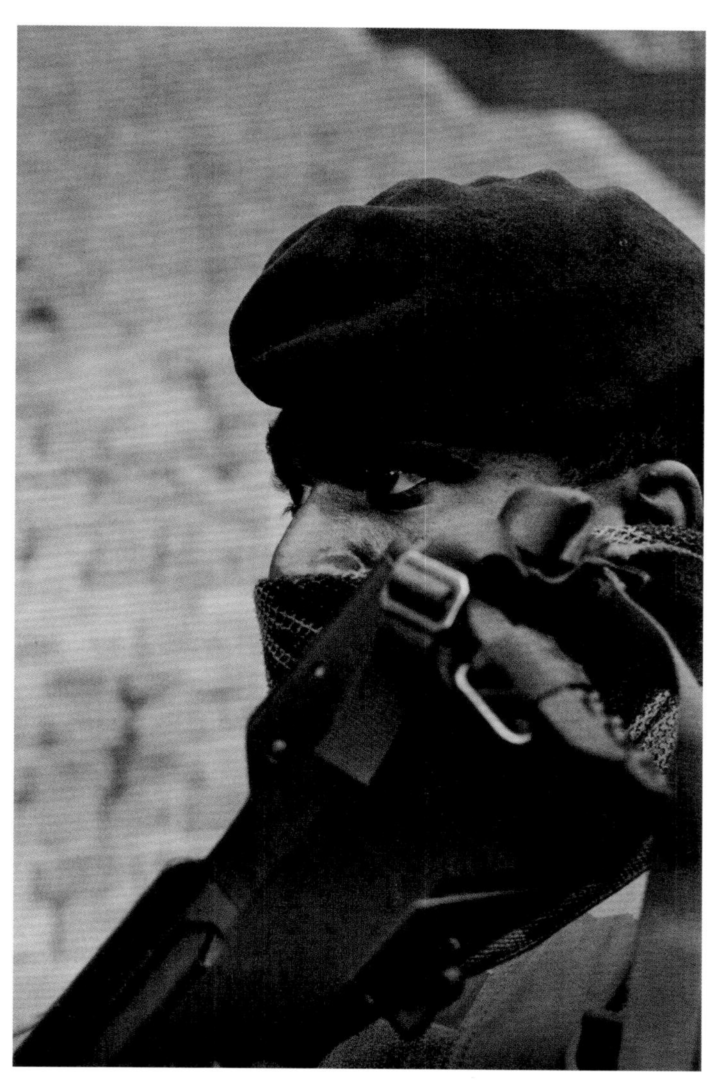

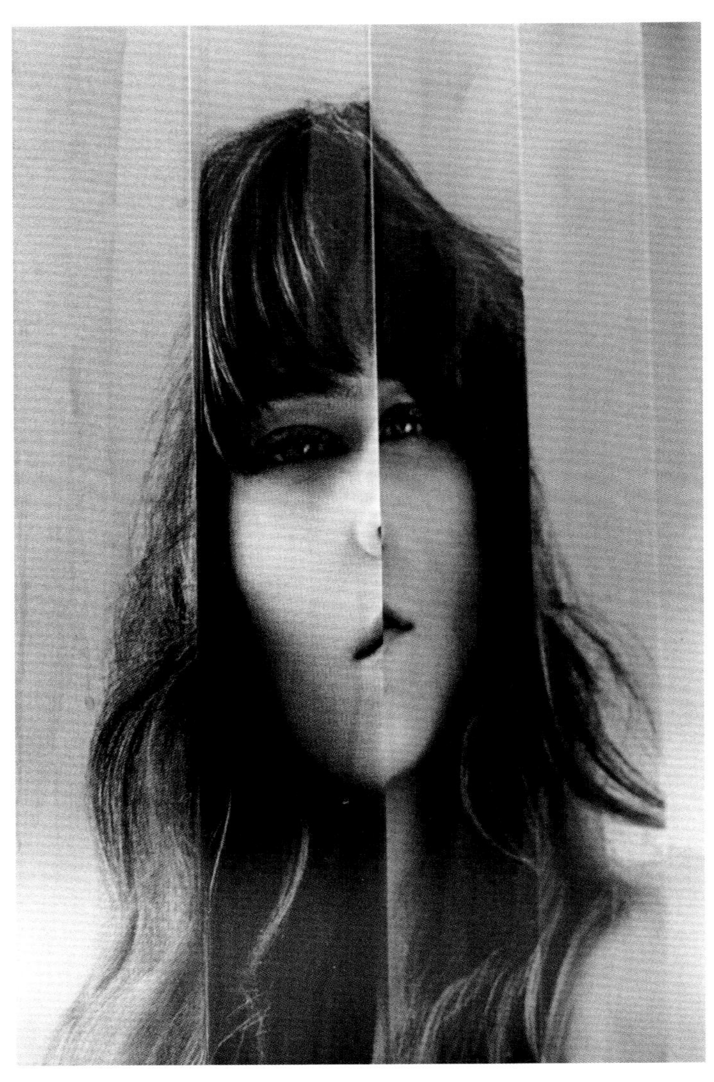

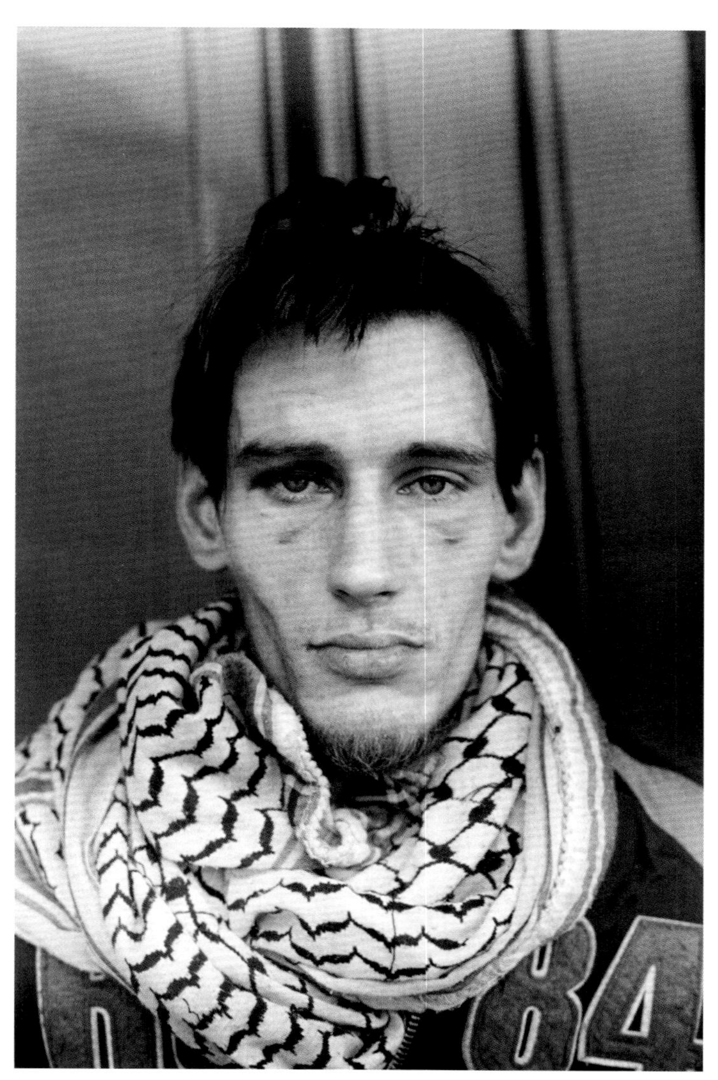

Rupert Frere

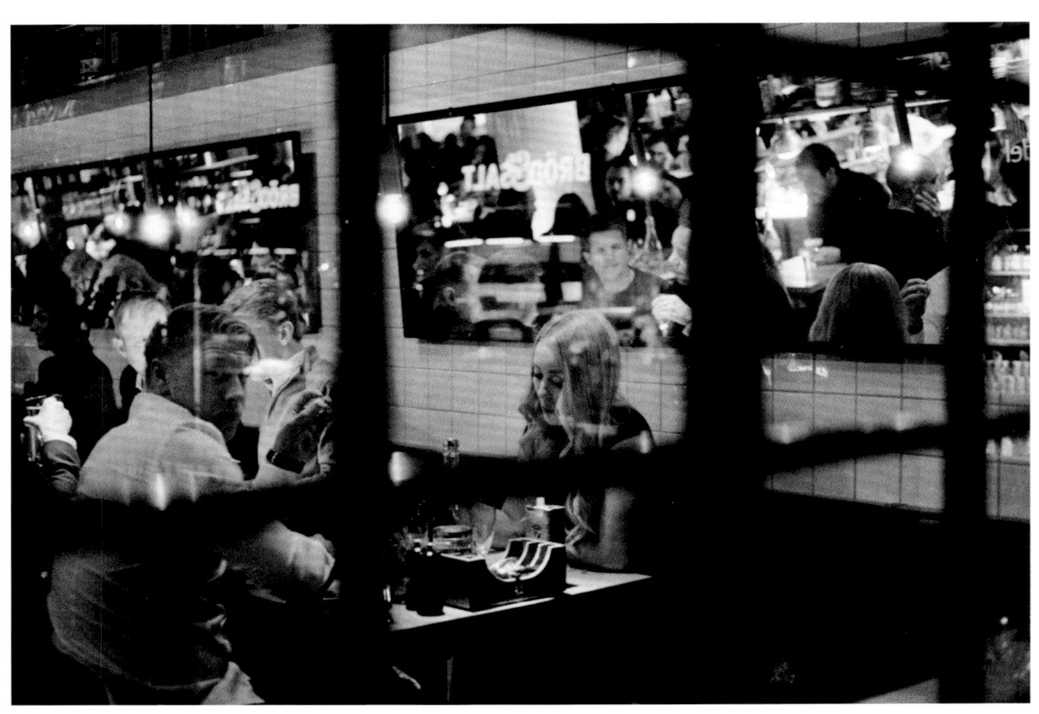

Yan Revazov

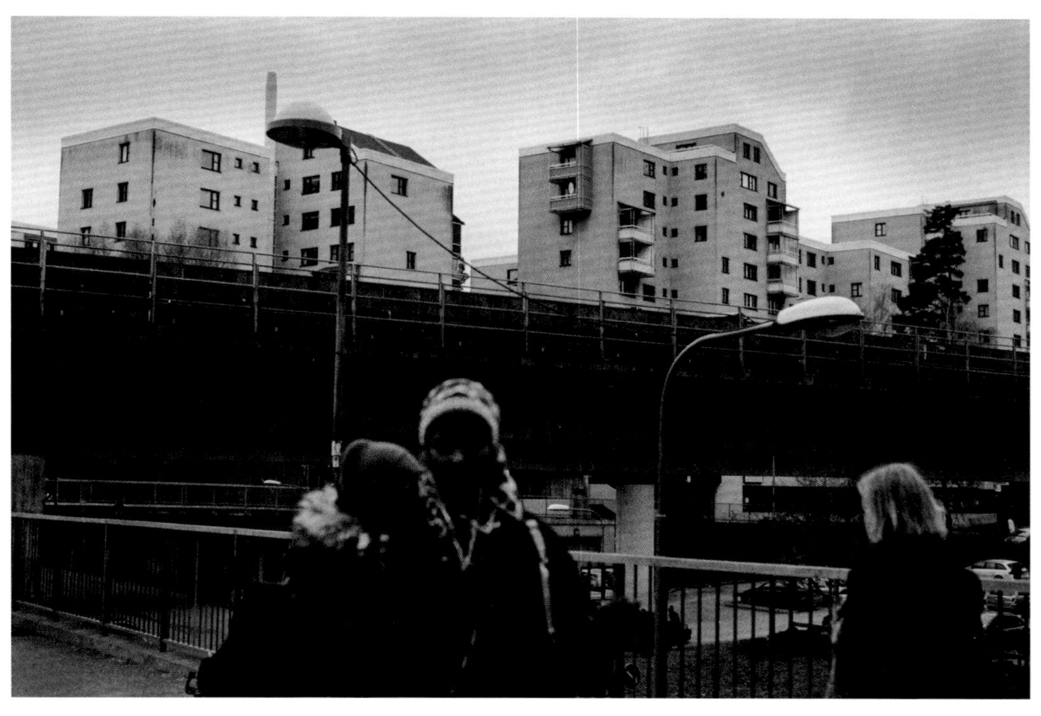

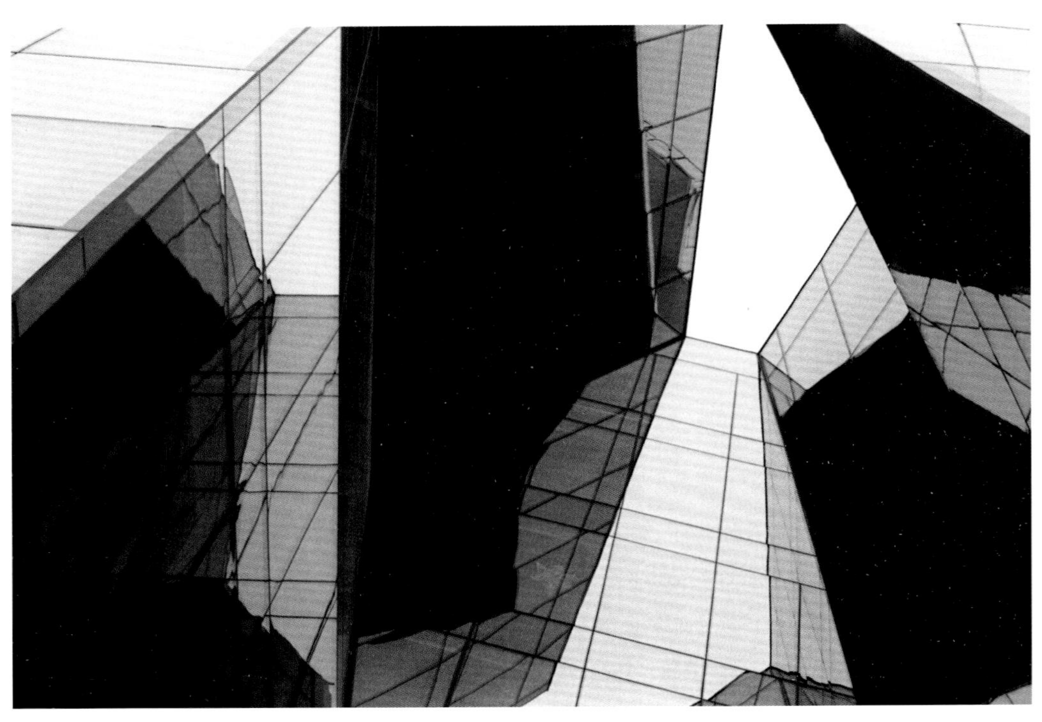

Yan Revazov

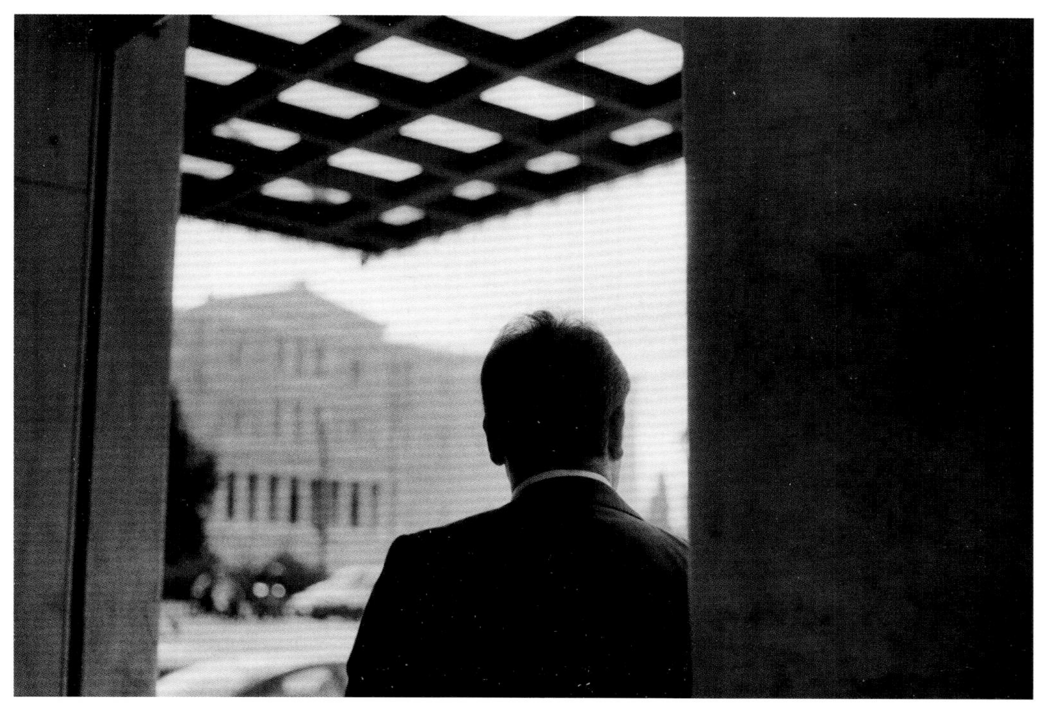

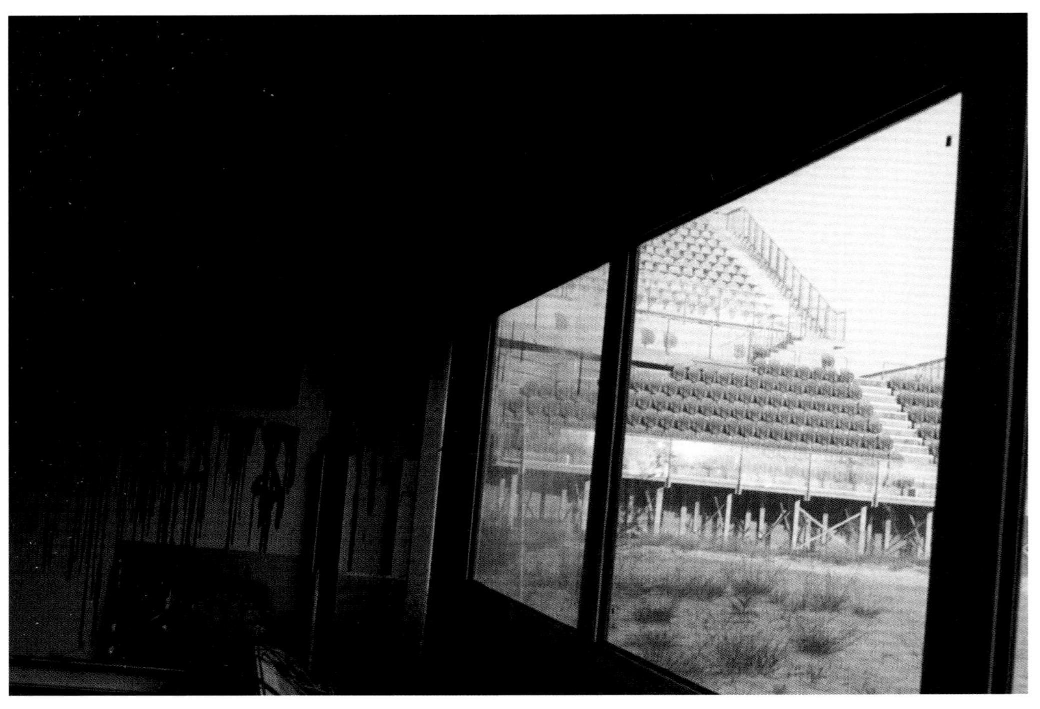

Marta Lallana García

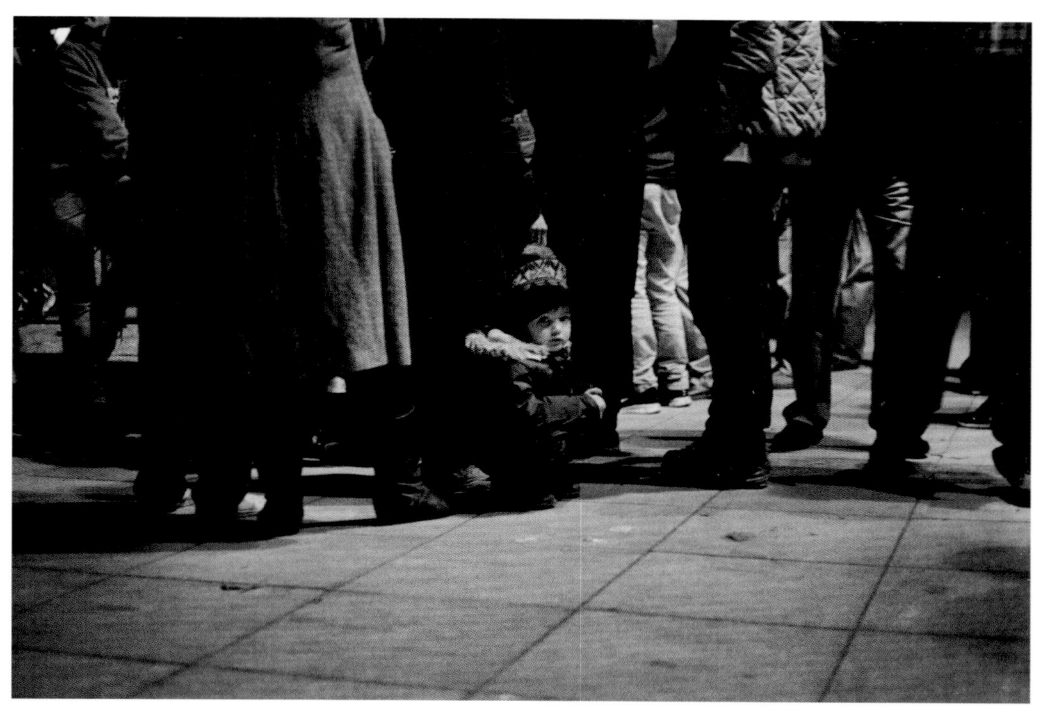

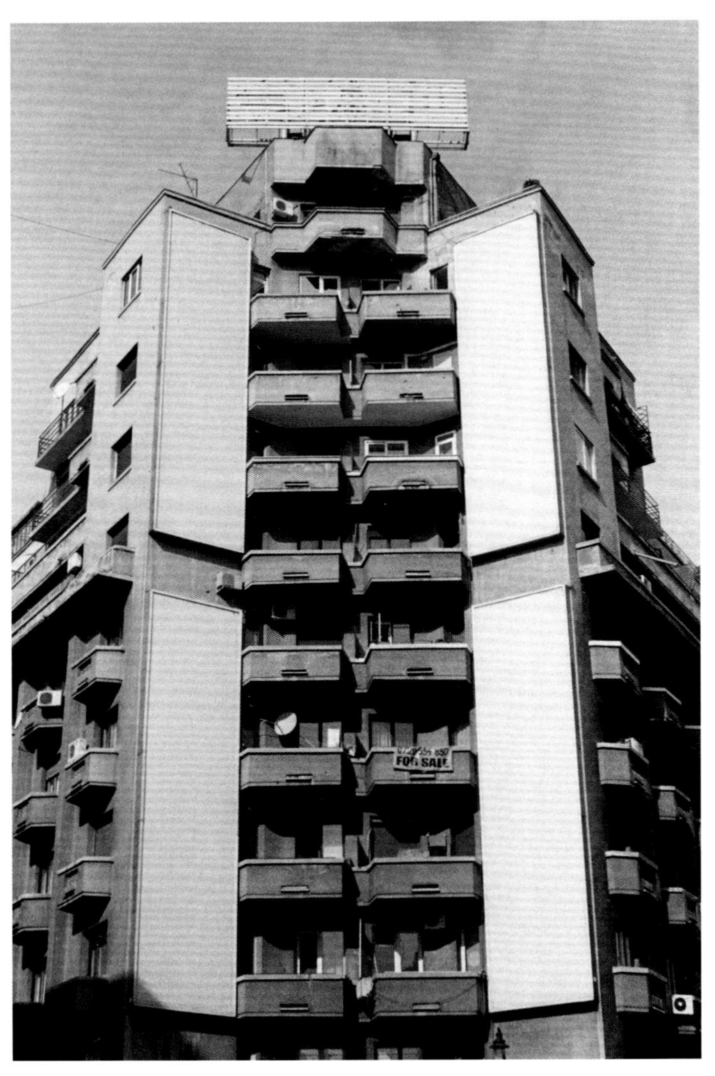

Gabriele Micalizzi

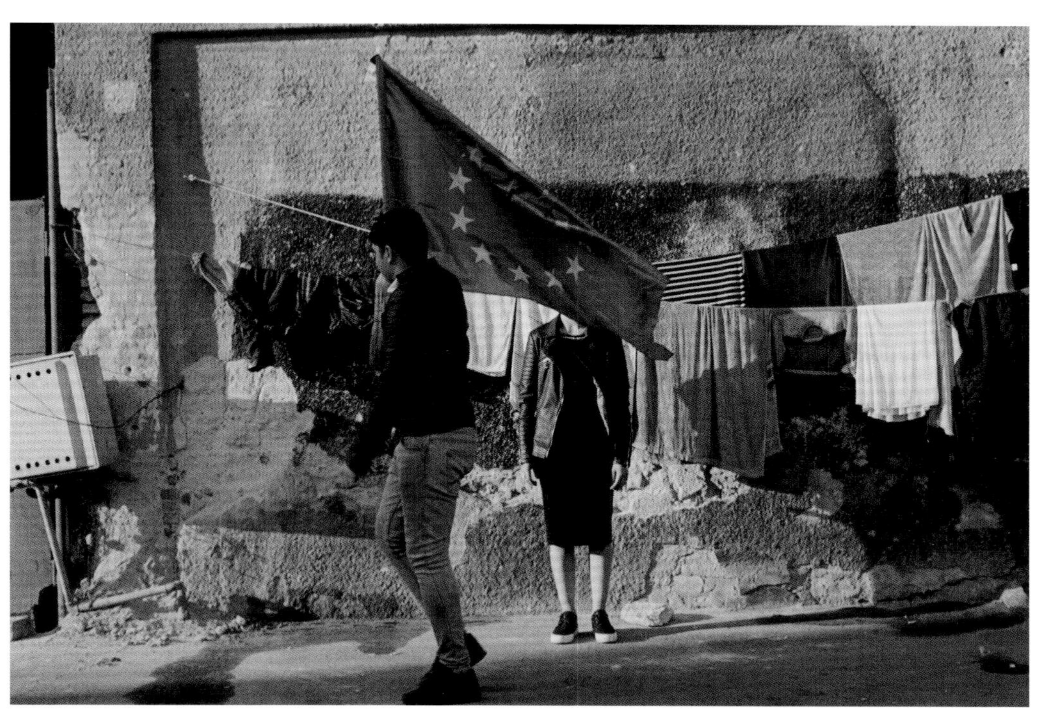

Gabriele Micalizzi

173

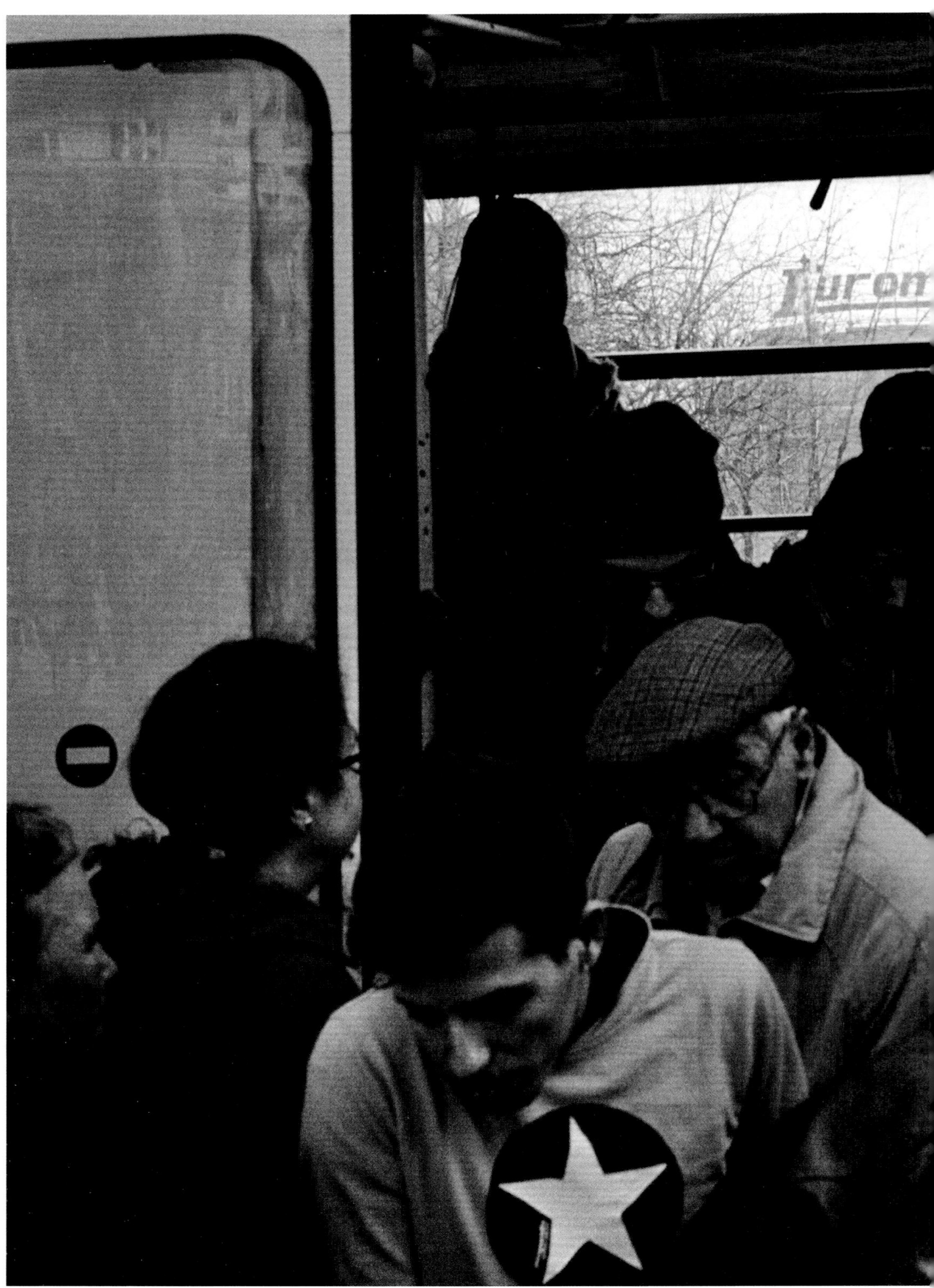
Turon

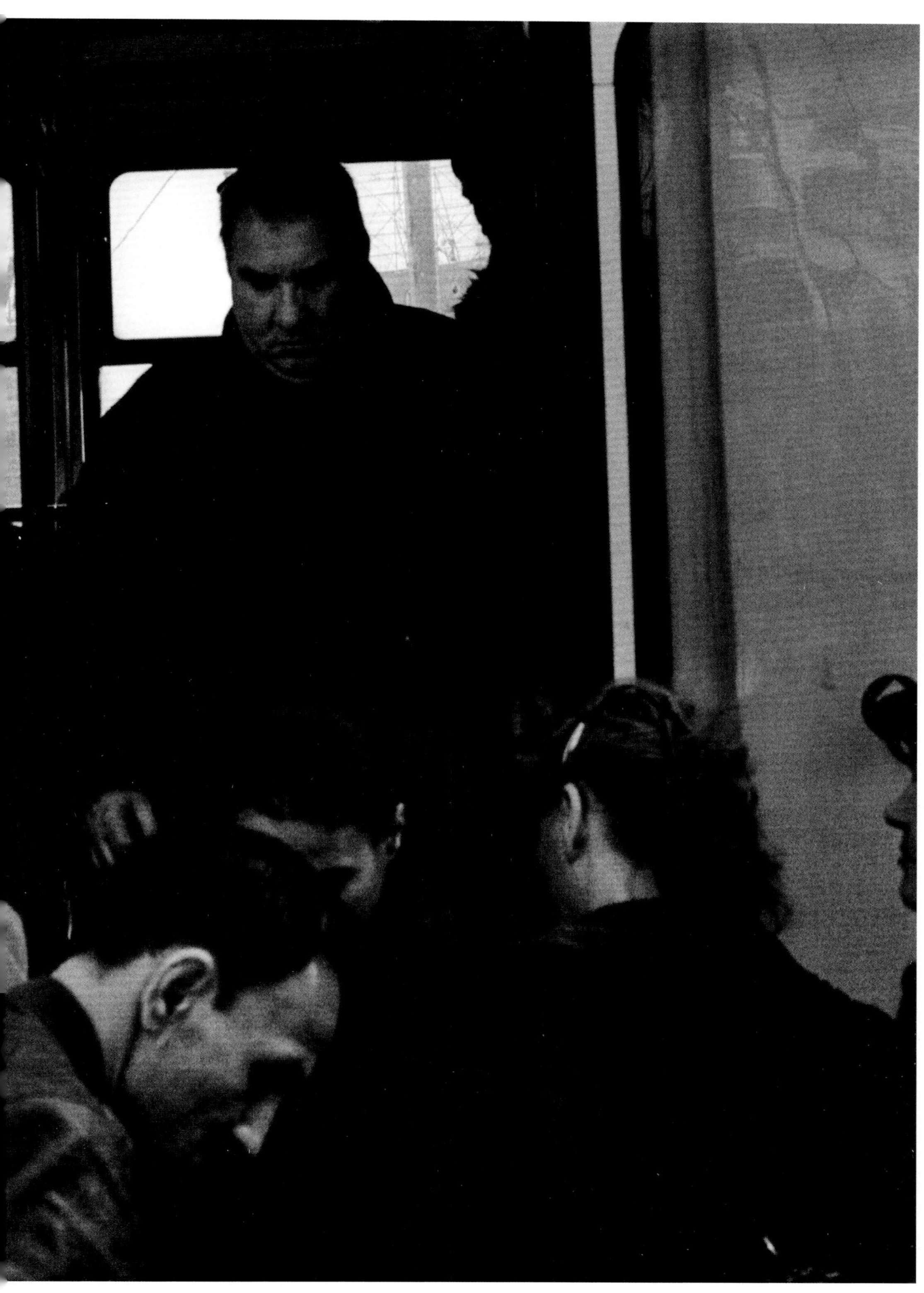